Teaching Geography Through Literature

Jack Papadonis
and
Wendy S. Wilson

J. WESTON
WALCH
PUBLISHER
Portland, Maine

User's Guide
to
Walch Reproducible Books

As part of our general effort to provide educational materials that are as practical and economical as possible, we have designated this publication a "reproducible book." The designation means that purchase of the book includes purchase of the right to limited reproduction of all pages on which this symbol appears:

Here is the basic Walch policy: We grant to individual purchasers of this book the right to make sufficient copies of reproducible pages for use by all students of a single teacher. This permission is limited to a single teacher, and does not apply to entire schools or school systems, so institutions purchasing the book should pass the permission on to a single teacher. Copying of the book or its parts for resale is prohibited.

Any questions regarding this policy or requests to purchase further reproduction rights should be addressed to:

Permissions Editor
J. Weston Walch, Publisher
321 Valley Street • P. O. Box 658
Portland, Maine 04104-0658

1   2   3   4   5   6   7   8   9   10
ISBN 0-8251-3824-8

Contents

Unit 3: *Julie of the Wolves* by Jean Craighead George

Unit 4: *Maroo of the Winter Caves* by Ann Turnbull

Unit 5: *Sarah, Plain and Tall* by Patricia MacLachlan

Unit 6: *The Captive* by Joyce Hansen

To the Teacher

For at least the past fifteen years, geography education has been of vital concern to parents and educators. National test scores indicate an increasing gap between American students' knowledge of the world and that of their counterparts in other countries. The infusion of geography instruction into the social studies curriculum has, thusly, assumed critical importance. Geography can and should be taught as a stand-alone course at the middle and high school levels. Additionally, integrating geographic concepts, skills, and standards into existing history, social science, and humanities courses is a viable means of addressing the issue of geographic literacy. To that end, using literature to teach geography provides stimulating and exciting opportunities to increase the presence of geography in students' academic lives.

Literature and geography make terrific partners. Literary works—be they poetry, novels, short stories, or non-fiction compositions—spark children's imaginations. Trade books also present information in a manner that can illustrate essential geographic concepts. Under teacher guidance, these concepts emerge through the discussion of the plot, characters, and setting of a literary work.

Choosing trade books or literary excerpts for classroom use involves some critical considerations. Does the composition relate to the concepts and content under examination in the geography course? Is the readability level appropriate for the students? Why is the book worth reading? Is it captivating and exciting to read?

Beyond direct curricular connections, trade books require further analysis. Good books exhibit care in their packaging. Inspect the book for the quality of the illustrations and sturdiness of the binding. Determine whether the text and illustrations match. There is nothing more confusing to students than for text and illustrations to be separated from each other by pages. Most important, ask yourself if the book is well written.

With this in mind, it is our purpose to present samples of literary works that can be linked to secondary-level social studies or history curricula with the goal of integrating geography concepts and skills. *Teaching Geography Through Literature* first introduces teachers and students to the national standards in geography and their attendant skills. While the activities included in this reproducible book are tied to specific literary compositions, they can be adapted to fit other literary, artistic, and musical works. Each of the activities brings into focus a particular geography standard coupled with geography skill work. Certainly, more than a single standard may be treated in a lesson, and you are encouraged to address multiple standards with any literary work.

The National Standards in Geography

The eighteen national standards in geography were developed under the auspices of four organizations: the American Geographical Society, the Association of American Geographers, the National Council for Geographic Education, and the National Geographic Society. The standards are organized around six essential elements that provide a systematic structure for the study of geography. *Geography for Life*, published by National Geographic Research and Exploration, clarifies in full detail each of the standards.

Element 1: The World in Spatial Terms

1. How to use maps and other geographic representations, tools, and technologies to acquire, process, and report information from a spatial perspective

2. How to use mental maps to organize information about people, places, and environments in a spatial context

3. How to analyze the spatial organization of people, places, and environments on Earth's surface

Element 2: Places and Regions

4. The physical and human characteristics of places

5. That people create regions to interpret Earth's complexity

6. How culture and experience influence people's perceptions of places and regions

Element 3: Physical Systems

7. The physical processes that shape the patterns of Earth's surface

8. The characteristics and spatial distribution of ecosystems on Earth's surface

Element 4: Human Systems

9. The characteristics, distribution, and migration of human populations on Earth's surface

10. The characteristics, distribution, and complexity of Earth's cultural mosaics

11. The patterns and networks of economic interdependence on Earth's surface

12. The processes, patterns, and functions of human settlement

13. How the forces of cooperation and conflict among people influence the division and control of Earth's surface

Element 5: Environment and Society

14. How human actions modify the physical environment

15. How physical systems affect human systems

16. The changes that occur in the meaning, use, distribution, and importance of resources

Element 6: The Uses of Geography

17. How to apply geography to interpret the past

18. How to apply geography to interpret the present and plan for the future

In addition to enumerating and defining the national standards, *Geography for Life* specifies "the geographic skills that a geographically informed person should have" (pp. 34–35). These skills are elaborated on thoroughly in the text (pp. 42–44):

1. Asking geographic questions

2. Acquiring geographic information

3. Organizing geographic information

4. Analyzing geographic information

5. Answering geographic questions

Teacher's Guide

Unit 1: *The Empty Pot* by Demi

Demi. *The Empty Pot.* New York: Henry Holt and Company, 1990.
(ISBN# 0-8050-1217-6)

Description

This is a story about a young Chinese boy's struggle to meet the emperor's challenge to grow the most beautiful flower in order to become the next emperor. Ping's endeavors throughout the year highlight this entertaining, yet powerful, story.

Classroom Applications

The story can be employed on many levels. Initially, it is a story about character and perseverance. It can be used to reinforce the values of hard work, honesty, and courage. Geographically, the story and accompanying illustrations can be used to bring the five Fundamental Themes and eighteen National Geography Standards into classroom instructional practice.

In addition to *The Empty Pot,* another book by Demi, *The Artist and the Architect,* is an excellent one to employ. Like *The Empty Pot,* this book has vivid illustrations and an engaging storyline.

There are numerous means of communicating the story to students. Two of the most common methods are to use the book as a read-aloud or to purchase multiple copies for use by students individually or in groups. The activities that follow demonstrate ways in which the book can be used.

To assist students through the book, have them complete a flowchart for the story as they read. This will help them to organize their thinking and keep track of the story's progress. The reproducible flowchart on page 3 can be photocopied for all students in your class for this purpose.

The Empty Pot Flowchart

Directions: Complete this flowchart for *The Empty Pot* as you read the book.

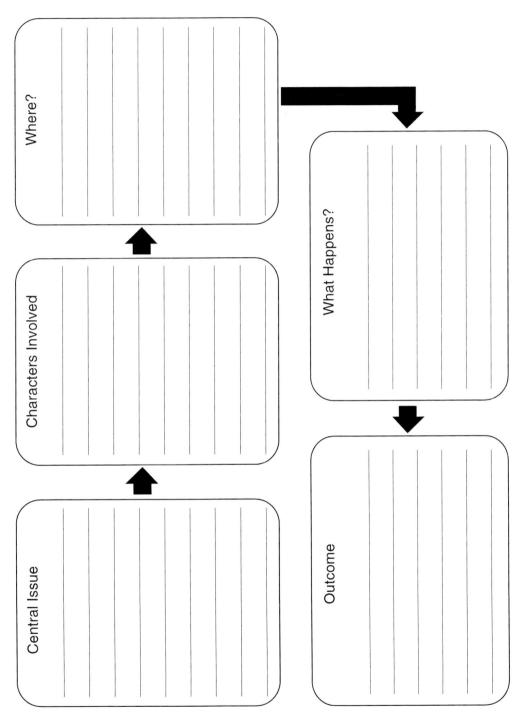

Where?

Characters Involved

Central Issue

What Happens?

Outcome

Teaching Geography Through Literature

Lesson 1: Where's China?

Teacher's
Lesson
Plan

I. **Time:** one class period (45 minutes)

II. **Frameworks/Standard Connection**

<u>Standard 1:</u> how to use maps and other geographic representations, tools, and technologies to acquire, process, and report information from a spatial perspective

<u>Standard 7:</u> the physical processes that shape the patterns of Earth's surface

<u>Standard 15:</u> how physical systems affect human systems

III. **Materials**

- pull-down world map; physical, population, and climate maps of China and the United States, or one class set of world atlases

- one class set of blank world maps; one class set of blank physical maps of China for students (pp. 6–7)

- one class set each of the What About China? and What's in China? student reproducible worksheets 1A and 1B

- colored pencils or crayons

IV. **Objectives—Students will be able to:**

- locate China on a world map

- identify/describe the distribution of population in China

- identify the climatic regions in China and compare them with students' own locale

- locate the major physical features and river systems in China

V. **Procedures**

1. Ask students what they know about China (location, culture, etc.).

2. Point out China's location in the world (locate by hemispheres, relative location to the United States, and local place). Distribute the blank world map. Then direct students to locate China, as well as China's neighboring countries and bodies of water, and to place them on their world maps.

3. Ask students to locate their place on their blank world map. Then have them use a climate map to determine their specific climate type.

4. Using a climate map of China, have students identify the various climate types found there. Lead the students in a question-and-answer session to establish similarities and differences between China and their locale. Have students complete the What About China? worksheet.

5. Distribute the What's in China? worksheet and blank physical map of China. Have students complete the activity.

Extension Activity Organize a Chinese folk fair as an extension of this story (or a unit on Asia). Students could arrange a display of folk/craft items such as dolls, jewelry, or clothing. Other items to include are stamps, coins, musical selections, and games. As part of the display, students could exhibit maps of the Chinese provinces and linguistic regions.

Name _____   Date _____

World Map

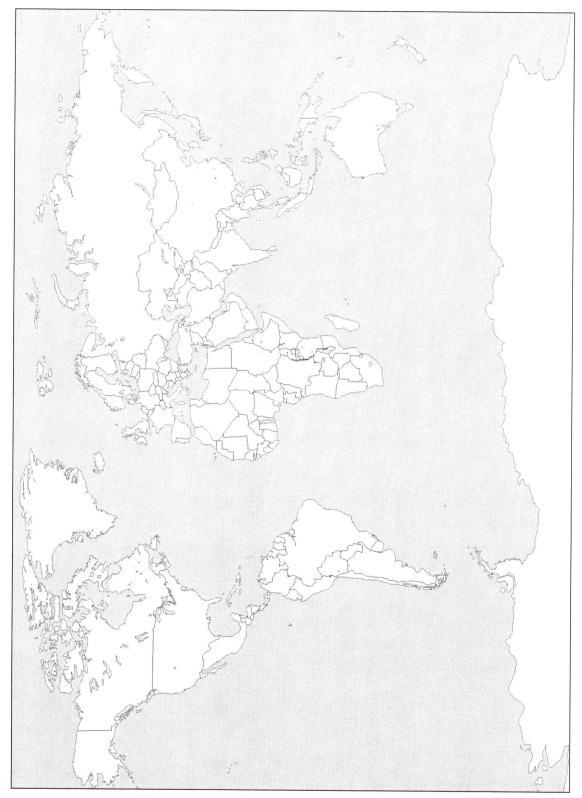

Name _____ Date _____

Physical Map of China

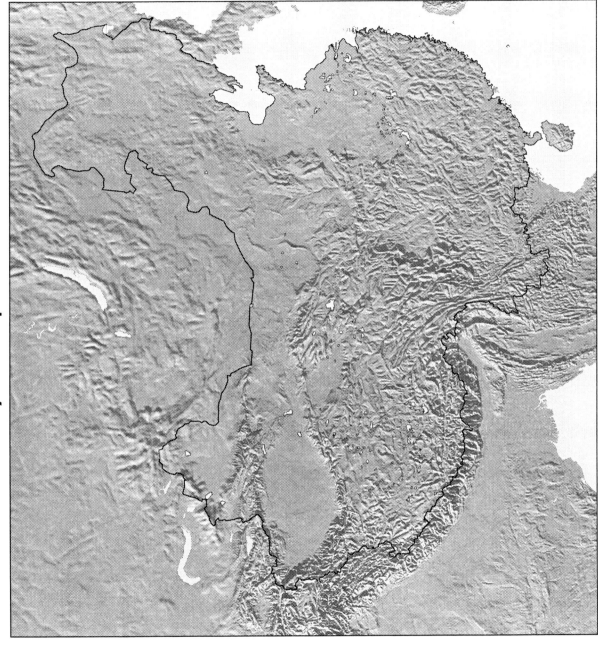

Name _____   Date _____

What About China?

 Directions: Use classroom maps of China showing climate, physical features, and population distribution to answer the following questions.

1. What are the major climate types found in China?

   _____

   _____

   _____

   _____

2. Where are these climate types found? Be as accurate and descriptive as possible.

   _____

   _____

   _____

   _____

3. Spend some time observing the population distribution in China. What patterns do you detect? Refer to the physical and climate maps. What additional observations can you deduce from this information?

   _____

   _____

   _____

   _____

What's in China?

 Directions: Locate the following places on the blank physical map of China.

Landforms	
Kunlun Mountains	Plateau of Tibet
Tien Shan	Gobi Desert
Himalaya Mountains	Taklimakan Desert
Mount Everest	Mount Godwin Austen (K2)
Qin-Lin Range	

Bodies of Water	
Grand Canal	Huang He
Yangtze River	Yalu River
Mekong River	Salween River
Brahmaputra River	

Lesson 2: *The Empty Pot*

I. **Time:** one class period (45 minutes)

II. **Frameworks/Standard Connection**

<u>Standard 7</u>: the physical processes that shape the patterns of Earth's surface

<u>Standard 8</u>: the characteristics and spatial distribution of ecosystems on Earth's surface

<u>Standard 9</u>: the characteristics, distribution, and migration of human populations on Earth's surface

<u>Standard 10</u>: the characteristics, distribution, and complexity of Earth's cultural mosaics

III. **Materials**

- *The Empty Pot* by Demi

- chart paper or transparency slides for recording student responses

- one class set of Physical and Human Characteristics student reproducible worksheet 2A

- drawing paper for student illustrations of local environment

IV. **Objectives—Students will be able to:**

- identify/describe the physical characteristics of a place

- identify/describe the human characteristics of a place

- gather information from narrative and illustrative material

V. **Procedures**

1. Introduce the book and storyline of *The Empty Pot*.

2. Tell students to note human and physical characteristics. (Half of the class can observe for one set; the other half can observe for the other.)

3. Gather students in the reading area or near the reader. Or, distribute multiple copies to students for individual or small-group reading.

4. Tell students to observe the illustrations as they hear the story.

5. Review vocabulary *(proclamation, emperor, successor, swarm)*.

6. Read the story, taking care that all students can view the illustrations.

7. While reading, ask questions. (Be sure to draw comparisons with your local climate and environment.) Possibilities include what students notice about:

   • the changing of the seasons

   • Ping's feelings

   • the Emperor's actions

8. At the conclusion, ask about the moral of the story.

9. Record student observations in categories.

10. Ask students to compare the physical and human characteristics exhibited in the story with their locale.

11. Summarize by restating the standards connections.

Extension Activity Have students draw pictures of their neighborhoods, illustrating its physical and human characteristics.

Name _____ Date _____

Physical and Human Characteristics

 Directions: Use this chart to record your observations of human and physical characteristics of the Emperor's kingdom.

Human Characteristics	Physical Characteristics

Extension Activities

To the Teacher

The purpose of these questions is to extend students' knowledge about Chinese culture and history. Geography, as we know, sets the context for studying about regions and countries. The topics listed below are a representative sample of the types of activities students can attempt.

Research Questions

1. How has China accommodated the large influx of population from rural areas to urban centers?

2. In June 1997, Hong Kong was returned to China after 99 years of British control. What changes has this return created for the people who live in Hong Kong? Hong Kong is also a major economic center in East Asia. How will the communist takeover affect trade relations with the United States, Japan, and the European Economic Community?

3. China has a formidable physical environment, much of which you identified in the What About China? and What's in China? worksheets. What conclusions can you draw from them in relation to population, agricultural activities, and industrialization? (*Helpful Hint:* Use the concepts of **resources** and **vegetation** to assist you.)

Other Resources for Teaching with *The Empty Pot*

Web Site

http://www.night.net/rosie/reading-list.html

This is an annotated reading list specifically about China (for both children and adults) with links to the Amazon on-line bookstore to purchase the listed books. This list was published especially for parents adopting children from China.

Teacher's Guide

Unit 2: *The Cay* by Theodore Taylor

Taylor, Theodore. *The Cay*. New York: Avon Books, 1969.

Description

This is a story concerning the awakening understanding of a young boy to the realities of humanity. Shipwrecked on an island and blinded by a blow to the head, Phillip discovers that the color of a man's skin is not the key to his nature. On the contrary, it is the acts of kindness he performs and the wisdom he imparts that are the reality.

Classroom Applications

The Cay is a classic novel that has implications for geography and social science instruction. Simply, as literature, it is profound in its message about humanity. The most appropriate use of this chapter book is through individual student reading. To that end, multiple classroom copies should be used to implement the accompanying lessons and activities. While the activities are not chapter specific, the teacher may choose to align them with particular sections of the book.

Because of the widespread acceptance of *The Cay,* Theodore Taylor has authored a prequel, *Timothy of The Cay.* This book, too, is a valuable addition to a literature-based geography curriculum. Some lessons make specific references to this book. However, students may respond using evidence from *The Cay.*

To assist students through the book, they should complete a flowchart for each chapter they read. This will help them to organize their thinking and keep track of the story's progress. The reproducible flowchart on page 16 can be photocopied for all students in your class for this purpose.

The Cay Flowchart

Directions: Complete this flowchart for each chapter of *The Cay* as you read the book.

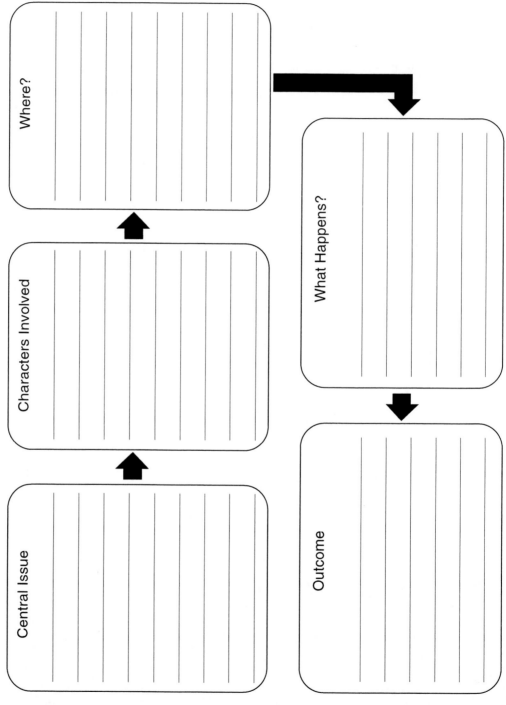

Where?

Characters Involved

Central Issue

What Happens?

Outcome

Lesson 1: Setting the Scene

I. **Time:** one class period (45 minutes)

II. **Frameworks/Standard Connection**

<u>Standard 1:</u> how to use maps and other geographic representations, tools and technologies to acquire, process, and report information from a spatial perspective

<u>Standard 2:</u> how to use mental maps to organize information about people, places, and environments in a spatial context

III. **Materials**

- pull-down world map showing Caribbean region, or one class set of world atlases

- class set of outline map of Latin America (p. 19)

- class sets of Locating Places and Where Are We? student reproducible worksheets 1A and 1B

- colored pens or pencils and rulers

- blank paper to create mental maps

- chart paper to record student responses during brainstorming session

IV. **Objectives—Students will be able to:**

- locate/identify specific Caribbean islands

- describe the route taken by the *S. S. Hato* from Curaçao

- draw sketch maps from memory to illustrate relative location, size, and distance

- calculate distance and direction on a map

V. **Procedures**

1. Prior to reading the novel, conduct a brainstorming session to access prior student knowledge of the Caribbean region. After listing as many responses as the students can offer, categorize the responses for organizational purposes. The categories can take many forms: language, landforms, products (*see Extension Activity on the following page*). Then have students look at the class pull-down map or their classroom atlases to confirm the geographic information elicited during the brainstorming session.

2. After reading the book, or at least the first two chapters, have students draw a sketch map of the Caribbean from memory. Once completed, have the students compare their sketch maps with their classroom map or atlases.

3. Distribute the Locating Places student worksheet and Latin America maps, and have students complete them as classwork or homework.

4. Pass out the Where Are We? student worksheet. Using their Latin American maps, students should complete the activity as classwork.

 **Extension Activity** Using the categories created during the brainstorming activity, divide the class into investigative learning teams. Assign a category to each team, and have them prepare an exhibition of their investigative results.

Name _____ Date _____

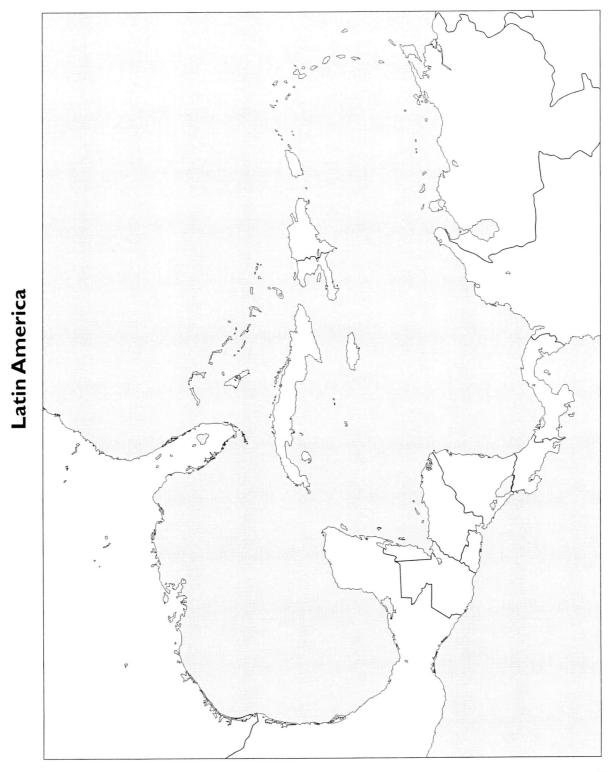

Latin America

Name _____   Date _____

Locating Places

 Directions: Use the outline map of Latin America to complete the following activity. Be sure to create a map key complete with all of its components.

1. Locate and label the following on your outline map:

Curaçao	Willemstad	Atlantic Ocean
Aruba	Lesser Antilles	Caribbean Sea
Venezuela	Caracas	Lake Maracaibo
Panama	Colon	Greater Antilles
Florida	Miami	Cuba
Hispaniola	Puerto Rico	Bahamas
Mexico	Pacific Ocean	Gulf of Mexico

2. Using a red pen or pencil, mark on your map what you think is the best sea route from Curaçao to Panama. Be sure to identify this symbol in your map key.

3. Using a green pen or pencil, mark on your map what you think would have been the best route for the *S.S. Hato* to have taken from Colon to Miami. Be sure to identify this symbol in your map key.

4. Using the scale, calculate the distance the *S.S. Hato* would have traveled following your routes.

Name _____   Date _____

Where Are We?

 Directions: Use the clues in Chapters 3 and 7 to complete the following questions. You will also need your map of Latin America.

1. **Define:**

Longitude	Latitude
Cay	Coral
Navigation	Devil's Mouth
Island	Bank

2. Mark on your Latin America map approximately where Timothy believes he and Philip have landed.

3. Why does Philip believe they will be on the island for a long time? Whom does he blame, and why?

Lesson 2: Different, But Similar

Teacher's Lesson Plan

I. **Time:** two class periods (45 minutes)

II. **Frameworks/Standard Connection**

Standard 9: the characteristics, distribution, and migration of human populations on Earth's surface

III. **Materials**

- pictures of people from magazines, newspapers, or like sources

- poster paper

- class set of What's Your Opinion? reproducible student worksheet 2A

IV. **Objectives—Students will be able to:**

- support opinions with evidence from their reading

- explain how skin color is the result of science and geographic location

V. **Procedures**

1. Make available to students a variety of magazines to cut pictures of people with different skin color. Students can work in groups or individually on this exercise.

2. Mount pictures on the classroom bulletin board or poster paper. After displaying the pictures, ask students to accurately describe the skin color of the people in each picture.

3. Initiate a discussion with students by asking:

   "How are these people the same?"

   "How are they different?"

   "Why is there such variation within the same skin color?"

4. Attitudes toward people often change. Students should complete the What's Your Opinion? student worksheet using evidence from the book to support their claims. This exercise may be implemented with the class individually or in groups with each group attacking a different question. Responses may be given orally or in a written essay. An adaptation of this activity is to treat the questions, especially #1, as debate resolutions. Students could form debate teams and marshall evidence from *The Cay, Timothy of the Cay,* or other appropriate sources.

Extension Activity If students cannot articulate an answer to the question, "Why is there such variation within the same skin color?", they should conduct research into the causes of skin color differences. The results of their research can be added to the bulletin board display.

What's Your Opinion?

 Directions: Based upon your reading of *The Cay* and, perhaps, *Timothy of the Cay*, please respond to these statements. Assert whether you agree or disagree, and support your claims with evidence from the book(s).

1. On page 150 of *Timothy of the Cay*, Philip's father states, "Wisdom comes in a lot of varieties." Is he correct?

   _____

   _____

2. "My father had always taught me to address anyone I took to be an adult as 'mister,' but Timothy didn't seem to be a mister. Besides, he was black." (page 35, *The Cay*)

   _____

   _____

3. What does Philip mean when he asks, "Timothy, are you still black?" (page 104, *The Cay*)

   _____

   _____

4. "Something happened to me that day on the cay. I'm not quite sure what it was even now, but I had begun to change. I said to Timothy, 'I want to be your friend'." Why does Philip's attitude toward Timothy change? (page 76, *The Cay*)

   _____

   _____

Lesson 3: Marooned

Teacher's Lesson Plan

I. **Time:** two to three class periods (45 minutes each)

II. **Frameworks/Standard Connection**

<u>Standard 4:</u> the physical and human characteristics of places

<u>Standard 7:</u> the physical processes that shape the patterns of Earth's surface

<u>Standard 8:</u> the characteristics and spatial distribution of ecosystems on Earth's surface

<u>Standard 11:</u> the patterns and networks of economic interdependence on Earth's surface *(see Extension Activity on the following page)*

III. **Materials**

- class set of atlases with resource and vegetation maps of the Caribbean

- two outline maps of the Caribbean area for each student (p. 27)

- class set of Island Resources student worksheet 3A

- class set of Survival student worksheet 3B

- class set of Natural Disasters student worksheet 3C

IV. **Objectives—Students will be able to:**

- identify the physical characteristics of Caribbean islands

- describe the effect of humans on the environment

- explain the effects of Earth's physical processes

- demonstrate the interdependence evident in the Caribbean *(see Extension Activity on the following page)*

V. **Procedures**

1. Introduce this lesson by addressing the concept of human and environmental interaction focusing on the physical characteristics of place. Use the local environment as an example.

2. Distribute classroom atlases and draw students' attention to maps that deal with the environment and resources of the Caribbean islands. Ask students questions concerning the distribution of resources, the natural vegetation, and the distribution of population in the Caribbean.

3. Hand out the two outline maps of the Caribbean Region. Instruct students to place the information from the atlases on their blank maps. Next, have them complete the Island Resources student worksheet.

4. Discuss with students the necessities for survival. What are the basic needs of humans in order to maintain life? List and categorize those that are met by the environment Timothy and Philip are confronted with. Then, have students complete the Survival student worksheet. As an alternative to reading answers aloud or engaging students in a class discussion of the Survival student worksheet, have students illustrate, role play, or perform their answers.

5. Timothy is killed during a violent storm (Chapter 15). Discuss with the students the different forms of natural disasters that can affect islands (tropical storms, tidal waves, earthquakes, volcanic eruptions, hurricanes). Students should complete the Natural Disasters student worksheet and prepare individual reports to the class.

 **Extension Activity** Develop a case study of this region by assigning different Caribbean islands to pairs or triads of students. The students will conduct research and organize their information using maps, charts, graphs, and pictures. Each case study should contain a narrative that illustrates the variety of land uses and economic activity for the island under study.

Caribbean Region

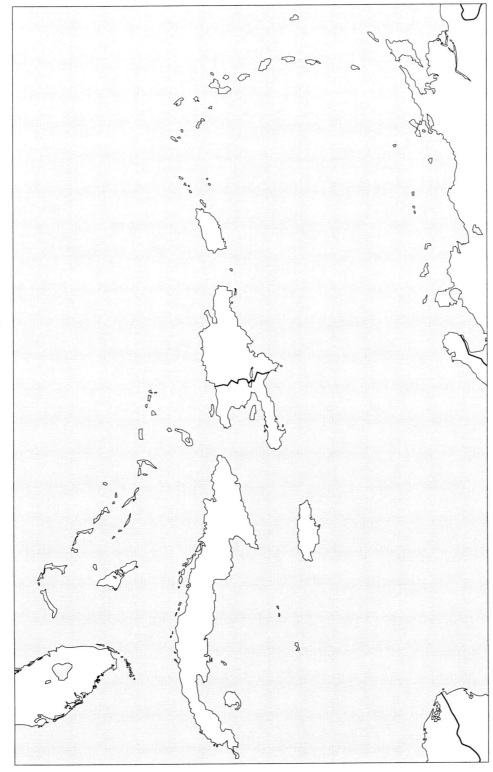

Teaching Geography Through Literature

Name _____   Date _____

Island Resources

 Directions: Use your classroom atlases to discover the resources, animals, and vegetation of Caribbean islands. After placing the information on your maps of the Caribbean Region, complete the chart below.

Animals	Vegetation	Natural Resources
_____	_____	_____
_____	_____	_____
_____	_____	_____
_____	_____	_____
_____	_____	_____
_____	_____	_____
_____	_____	_____
_____	_____	_____
_____	_____	_____

◆ What items from the lists above are mentioned in *The Cay*?

_____

_____

_____

_____

Survival

 Directions: Based upon your research from the Island Resources worksheet and your reading of *The Cay*, respond to the questions below.

1. Describe the ecosystem of the cay that Timothy and Philip are on.

   _____

   _____

   _____

2. How did Timothy use the environment to ensure Philip's and his survival?

   _____

   _____

3. Evaluate the impact of Timothy and Philip's presence on the environment. What evidence do you have to support your conclusions?

   _____

   _____

   _____

4. **Prediction:** What would happen to the environment if the island became accessible to vessels and a resort was established?

   _____

   _____

   _____

Natural Disasters

 Directions: This is a research-centered project. You will compile a report on natural disasters that have affected one or more of the Caribbean islands. You may use newspapers, magazines, videos, or historical records to obtain your information. The report can deal with recent disasters or ones from history. Respond to the first question before you start your research.

1. How did Timothy prepare for the oncoming storm?

_____

_____

_____

_____

2. Choose a natural disaster that has impacted a Caribbean island. Research its causes and effects. Pay specific attention to the alteration, if any, of the physical characteristics of the island. Next, assess its effect on the human population. In your reporting, be sure to focus on ways in which natural processes contribute to environmental damage and problems. Use the space below for notes.

_____

_____

_____

_____

_____

_____

Other Resources for Teaching with *The Cay* and *Timothy of the Cay*

Books

Butzow, Carol M. and John W. *Intermediate Science Through Children's Literature: Over Land and Sea.* Teacher Ideas Press, Englewood, CO, 1994. ISBN 0-87287-946-1. Contains science lessons based upon *Julie of the Wolves, Sarah, Plain and Tall,* and *The Cay,* as well as other well-known books.

Web Sites

http://vega.lib.vt.edu/ejournals/ALAN/fall95/Ericson.html

A site titled "At Home With Multicultural Literature," it focuses on the home as an important part of life in all cultures. The site has books and suggestions for their classroom use; it recommends *Timothy of the Cay* as an appropriate book to use. Written by Bonnie Ericson, who teaches in the Department of Secondary Education at California State University, Northridge.

http://www.ag.uiuc.edu/~disaster/csndact7.html

Contains a unit from the University of Illinois at Urbana-Champaigne titled "Children, Stress, and Natural Disaster." This unit was done for FEMA (Federal Emergency Management Agency) and uses *The Cay* and other activities to defuse stress in children who have experienced a natural disaster such as a hurricane or flood.

Media

There was a made-for-TV movie based upon *The Cay,* which starred James Earl Jones as Timothy. This Hallmark Hall of Fame production has never been distributed and is not presently available for purchase or rental. You may wish to check your local school or public library to see if someone there off-air taped and licensed this program to keep. With new videos being released frequently, it is a good idea to occasionally check a good educational media catalog such as Zenger Media to see if this video has been released.

George, Jean Craighead. *Julie of the Wolves.* New York: HarperCollins Children's Books, 1972. (ISBN# 0-06-021943-2)

Description

This novel is one of the best accounts focusing on relationships between people and the natural environment. This is a story about a young Eskimo girl who runs away from home and her trials to survive on the Alaskan tundra. It is her bonding with wolves that allows Julie to survive. There is great merit in her association with the wolves beyond subsistence. Loyalty is one lesson, as is respect for the harsh environment. The story continues through the sequels, *Julie* and *Julie's Wolfpack. Julie* tells the story of Miyax's return to her home and examines the relationships among Julie, her father, her step-mother, and the wolves. In *Julie's Wolfpack,* the focus is primarily on Alaskan wolves, the same pack introduced in the first volume.

Classroom Applications

While student worksheets specifically address the content contained in *Julie of the Wolves,* the sequel, *Julie,* may be used in its place. Indeed, reading groups could be established to treat all three books in class. With some alteration, most, if not all, of the following lessons and activities will apply to whatever novel is used. This process is a recommended methodology for employing literature in the geography classroom.

It is assumed that teachers will review sections of the book as students conduct their reading. All activities lend themselves to either direct teacher instruction or student completion and review.

To assist students through book, they should complete a flowchart for each chapter they read. This will help them to organize their thinking and keep track of the story's progress. The reproducible flowchart on the following page can be photocopied for all students in your class for this purpose.

Julie of the Wolves Flowchart

Directions: Complete this flowchart for each chapter of *Julie of the Wolves* as you read the book.

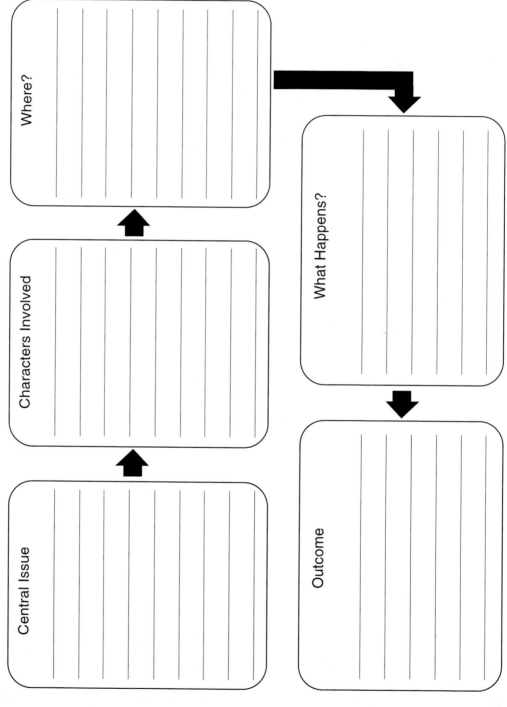

Where?

Characters Involved

Central Issue

What Happens?

Outcome

Lesson 1: The Grabber

I. **Time:** one class period for investigation and one class period for implementation (45 minutes each)

II. **Frameworks/Standard Connection**

Standard 6: how culture and experience influence people's perceptions of places and regions

III. **Materials**

- five shoe boxes

- Eskimo doll, sugar cubes, uniform lengths of sticks and pieces of material, walrus/seal/whale doll, and fish-shaped crackers

- one copy of The Boxes (reproducible student worksheet 1A) for each box

- chart paper and markers

IV. **Objectives—Students will be able to:**

- interpret cultural symbols

- make inferences and draw conclusions about Eskimo life and culture

V. **Procedures**

1. A few days prior to the activity, set out the five boxes, each containing one of the items listed above. The boxes should be sealed and tied with a student worksheet appended for students to record their guesses. Allow the boxes to be handled but not opened.

2. Brainstorm with students about their attitudes toward Eskimo people. Ask, "When you think of Eskimos, what comes into your mind first?"

3. Open the boxes. On chart paper, write the five items contained within. Try to match items with the brainstorming activity. Compare the items with student guesses. Were any guesses correct? How do students feel about these items?

4. Initiate a class discussion by stating, "The things you have found represent or symbolize some of the discoveries or items that were important to the Eskimo people for their culture and survival." Ask students what each item represents and why it might have been important to the Eskimos.

The Boxes

 Directions: Try to determine the contents of this box. You may shake and listen to the contents or weigh the box. You cannot open it. After thinking about what you have observed, record your guess as to the box's contents.

_____

_____

_____

_____

_____

_____

_____

_____

_____

_____

_____

_____

_____

Lesson 2: Amaroq, the Wolf

Teacher's
Lesson
Plan

I. **Time:** three class periods (45 minutes each)

II. **Frameworks/Standard Connection**

Standard 4: the physical and human characteristics of places

Standard 8: the characteristics and spatial distribution of ecosystems on Earth's surface

Standard 15: how physical systems affect human systems

III. **Materials**

- class set of Julie's Environment worksheet 2A

- chart paper for brainstorming activity

- pull-down world map, globe, and overhead projector

IV. **Objectives—Students will be able to:**

- identify and describe the Alaskan environment

- locate physical and human features on a map of Alaska

- explain the relationship between Eskimos and their environment

V. **Procedures**

1. Prior to reading Part I, *Amaroq, the Wolf,* conduct a brainstorming activity with students. Create a list of natural items that exist in our environment. Encourage students to be as specific as possible. After categorizing the list, students should read Part I.

2. Distribute the Julie's Environment student worksheet and have students complete it as they read. Assign different sections of the student worksheet depending on your nightly reading requirements. Each day in class, a review of the questions is necessary.

3. When students have completed the worksheet, they should each write an essay comparing Julie's environment with the local environment. Students should use the brainstorming activity list as a source of information and structure for their essays.

Julie's Environment

 Directions: As you read *Amaroq, the Wolf*, complete this activity.

1. From the reading, list some adjectives that describe Julie's environment.

   _____

   _____

2. Using examples from Part I, explain how humans have adapted to the Alaskan environment.

   _____

   _____

   _____

3. Identify these words:

   ulo _____

   kuspuck _____

   ilaya _____

   amaroq _____

   gussak _____

   ookpick _____

   (continued)

Julie's Environment *(continued)*

4. How did Julie learn about relating to the natural environment? In your answer, use specific examples from Part I.

_____

_____

_____

_____

_____

5. On page 55, what does Julie mean when she thinks, "She sniffed too, but for her the pages were blank"?

_____

_____

_____

_____

6. What clues did Julie "read" in the environment to tell her that the season is about to change? What are the clues in our environment that foretell a change from summer to autumn?

_____

_____

_____

_____

_____

Julie's Environment *(continued)*

7. In the chart below, record the animal and plant life found in Julie's environment.

Animal Life (fauna)	Plant Life (flora)

Lesson 3: The Land of Alaska

Teacher's Lesson Plan

I. **Time:** one class period (45 minutes)

II. **Frameworks/Standard Connection**

Standard 1: how to use maps and other geographic representations, tools, and technologies to acquire, process, and report information from a spatial perspective

III. **Materials**

- overhead projector and transparency of map of Alaska

- two class sets of blank Alaska maps (p. 42)

- classroom atlases

- class set of A Mapping Exercise reproducible student worksheet 3A

IV. **Objectives—Students will be able to:**

- identify and locate physical and human features of Alaska

- read and interpret symbols on a map

- determine the physical and climatic environment of the Eskimo

V. **Procedures**

1. This lesson can be done in conjunction with lesson 2, Amaroq, the Wolf.

2. Distribute maps and A Mapping Exercise worksheets to students. If this is to be done as classwork, also distribute classroom atlases.

3. When students have finished constructing their maps, have them approximate Miyax's relative location in Alaska.

Extension Activity Construct and compare climographs of Juneau, Fairbanks, and your own place on Earth. You will need to find the monthly precipitation and temperature rates for one calendar year for each location.

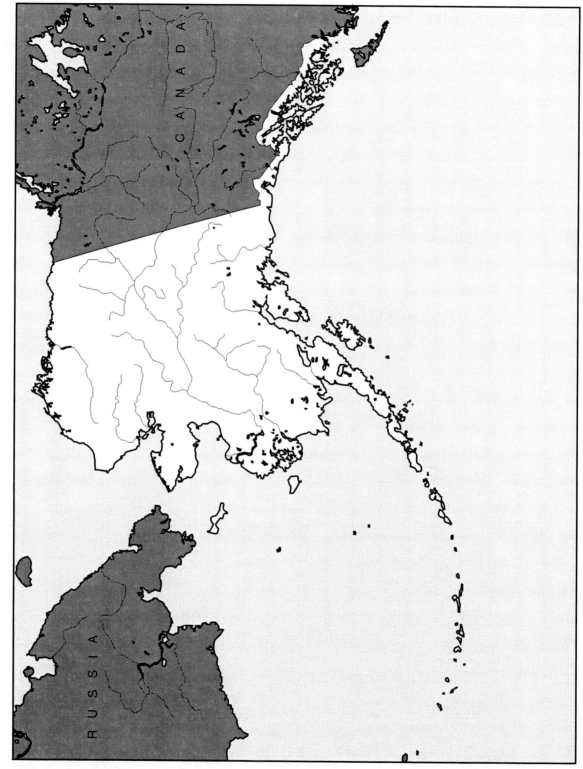

Alaska

A Mapping Exercise

1. Locate the following human and physical features on the blank map of Alaska. You may have to consult sources other than an atlas to complete this section.

    Point Barrow   Canada

    Bering Strait   Aleutian Islands

    Arctic Ocean   Mount McKinley

    Point Hope   Gulf of Alaska

    Fairbanks   Pacific Ocean

    Brooks Range   Route of the Alaskan Pipeline

    Bering Sea   Location of Gold Discoveries

2. Using a second blank map of Alaska, create a climate map. Include the following climates on your map.

    Tundra   Marine West Coast

    Taiga   Highland Climate

3. After comparing the two maps relative to the location of Fairbanks, what inferences can you draw about the advantages of its location? What are the disadvantages of its location?

Lesson 4: Miyax, the Girl

I. **Time:** one to three class periods (45 minutes each)

II. **Frameworks/Standard Connection**

   <u>Standard 6:</u> how culture and experience influence people's perceptions of places and regions

   <u>Standard 7:</u> the physical processes that shape the patterns of Earth's surface

   <u>Standard 10:</u> the characteristics, distribution, and complexity of Earth's cultural mosaics

III. **Materials**

   • Alaska maps from prior lesson

   • class set of The Eskimo's World reproducible student worksheet 4A

IV. **Objectives—Students will be able to:**

   • locate human and physical features on a map of Alaska

   • make inferences about Eskimo culture

V. **Procedures**

   1. Introduce additional map locations (Nome, Mekoryuk, Nash Harbor) and have students add them to their Alaska maps.

   2. Add *i'noGo tied* and *mukluk* to student vocabulary list.

   3. After students have completed Part II, *Miyax, the Girl* (or concurrently with their reading), distribute The Eskimo's World student worksheet. Students may complete this in class or for homework. You should review their observations with them. There should be a rich discussion focusing on the first question. Advise students to include additional supporting data from novel beyond the Bladder Feast.

The Eskimo's World

 Directions: After reading *Miyax, the Girl*, answer the following questions. Then complete the activity by addressing the last two items on this page.

1. What is the significance of the Bladder Feast? What does it tell of the Eskimos' relationship with nature? *(page 77)*

   _____

   _____

   _____

2. How could the Eskimos use the Sun and the moon to determine that Earth is round? *(page 85)*

   _____

   _____

   _____

3. Why do you think many of the men like Naka (a singer at seal camp) abuse alcohol? *(page 99)*

   _____

   _____

   _____

   Add to your map: Nome, Mekoryuk, Nash Harbor

   Add to your vocabulary: mukluk, i'noGo tied

Lesson 5: Seasons

I. **Time:** one class period (45 minutes)

II. **Frameworks/Standard Connection**

Standard 6: how culture and experience influence people's perceptions of places and regions

Standard 7: the physical processes that shape the patterns of Earth's surface

Standard 10: the characteristics, distribution, and complexity of Earth's cultural mosaics

III. **Materials**

- one large (16") globe representing Earth, one overhead projector representing the Sun

- class set of the The Seasons Vocabulary and Earth and the Sun reproducible student worksheets 5A and 5B

IV. **Objectives—Students should be able to:**

- describe the relationship between Earth and the Sun relating to seasons

- relate how some cultures explain natural phenomena

V. **Procedures**

1. After students have read through page 101 in Part II of *Julie of the Wolves*, conduct an in-class demonstration of the relationship between Earth and the Sun. The intent of the demonstration is to enable students to visualize the movement of Earth around the Sun.

2. Distribute The Seasons Vocabulary student worksheet for homework (or classwork) the day before the activity. Students should complete the vocabulary exercise, and you should establish common definitions for the class to use.

3. Using the diagram below as a guide, have students fill out the Earth and the Sun worksheet. They can follow your oral instructions to complete their diagrams and label them appropriately.

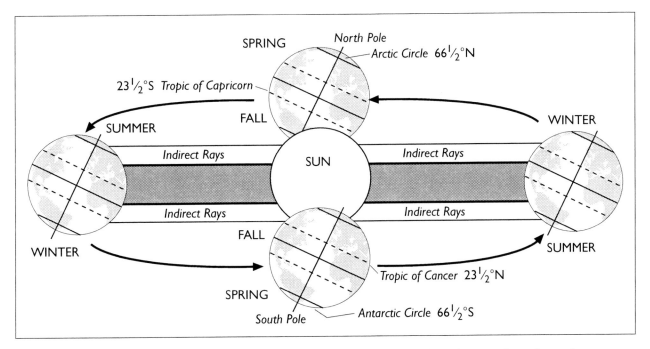

4. **Teacher Background Information:** Point out to the class that Earth is always in movement and is always tilted toward, away from, or neutral relative to the Sun. It is this movement that causes the seasons and changes in the amount of daylight and darkness on Earth. The two most critical movements are **rotation** and **revolution**. Rotation is the spinning of Earth on its axis (23.5), while revolution is the movement of Earth around the Sun. At different times of the year, the Sun's direct rays strike at specific places on Earth within the low latitudes (23.5 N–23.5 S). During the vernal and autumnal equinoxes, they strike on the equator. On the first day of summer in the Northern Hemisphere, they strike at the Tropic of Cancer (23.5 N). Near the poles, the areas defined by the Arctic and Antarctic Circles experience 24 hours of either daylight or darkness during the time of the solstices.

5. You can integrate math into this lesson by using Earth's tilt (23.5), the address of the poles (90 N or S), and the equator (0). When you perform the operation (90.0–23.5), the result is 66.5, which happens to be the signature of the Arctic (66.5 N) and Antarctic (66.5 S) Circles. Likewise, performing the operation (0+23.5) results in the location of the Tropics (23.5 N or S).

6. To demonstrate these relationships, place a large globe in the center of a darkened room. Using the overhead projector as the Sun, simulate Earth's orbit by turning the globe's axis to the positions indicated on the preceding diagram. The globe does not need to travel around the "Sun"; pointing the North Pole in different directions will accomplish the same purpose. During the demonstration, point out the conditions the "Sun" creates on the globe. Students, who should be standing behind the "Sun," will be able to see a bright spot of light representing the Sun's direct rays. These rays will "travel" within the low latitudes depending on the positioning of the globe. Similarly, the arctic or antarctic will be in total light or total darkness. This concrete, effective demonstration will allow students to articulate their knowledge about Earth-Sun relationships.

Extension Activity

1. After completing the Earth and the Sun exercise, assign students to write an essay describing the process.

2. Have students gather sunrise/sunset data from different cities in the world: e.g., their locality; Boston; Fairbanks; Cairo, Egypt; Quito, Ecuador; Sydney, Australia; and, if possible, an Antarctic Research Station. Students can graph this data and make comparisons among the cities.

Name _____ Date _____

The Seasons Vocabulary

 Directions: Using a dictionary or the glossary of a geography book, find the definitions of the following words as they apply to physical geography.

direct rays of the Sun _____

indirect rays of the Sun _____

axis _____

rotation _____

revolution _____

tilt _____

hemisphere _____

equator _____

equinox _____

prime meridian _____

Arctic Circle _____

Antarctic Circle _____

Tropic of Cancer _____

Tropic of Capricorn _____

(continued)

The Seasons Vocabulary *(continued)*

low latitudes _____

middle latitudes _____

high latitudes _____

tropics _____

temperate zone _____

polar regions _____

orbit _____

day _____

night _____

seasons _____

Circle of Illumination _____

dawn _____

dusk _____

solstice _____

Earth and the Sun

 Directions: Complete the diagram below.

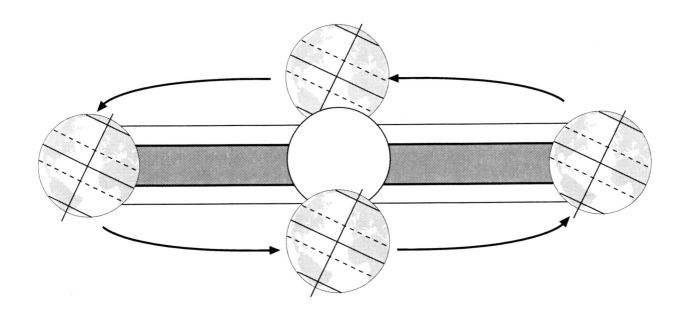

Lesson 6: Kapugen, the Hunter

I. **Time:** two to three class periods (45 minutes each)

II. **Frameworks/Standard Connection**

Standard 10: the characteristics, distribution, and complexity of Earth's cultural mosaics

III. **Materials**

- class set of Reflections reproducible student worksheet 6A

- overhead transparency and class set of the poem *Day and Night and How They Came To Be* (worksheet 6B)

IV. **Objectives—Students will be able to:**

- make inferences about Eskimo culture

- describe how Eskimos interpreted natural phenomena

V. **Procedures**

1. After students have completed *Kapugen, the Hunter,* they should complete the Reflections worksheet. The two questions should serve as powerful discussion openers. Students can draw from the whole novel to respond.

2. Distribute the poem *Day and Night and How They Came To Be.* Display the poem using an overhead projector. Using a series of questions, analyze the poem:

"What kind of fox is described in the poem?" (arctic fox)

"What color would that fox be?" (white in winter)

"What kind of hare lives in the Arctic?" (snowshoe)

"Why would the fox want to hunt in the dark?"

"Why do you think the Eskimo people believed that day and night were caused by a fox and a hare?"

"What does this poem say about the relationship between the Eskimo and nature?"

Extension Activity Extend the lesson by having students create their own poems using animals to explain natural phenomena.

Reflections

Directions: This last section of *Julie of the Wolves* brings into focus Miyax's conflicting feelings about traditional Eskimo culture and what has replaced it. Consider the two questions that follow.

1. What does Miyax mean when she says, "The old Eskimo customs are not so foolish—they have purpose. I'm as warm as the center of a lemming's nest"? What is the purpose of tradition and customs? *(page 126)*

    _____

    _____

    _____

    _____

    _____

    _____

2. At the conclusion of the novel, Miyax sings a song to Amaroq. Explain the meaning of, "That the hour of the wolf and the Eskimo is over." *(page 170)*

    _____

    _____

    _____

    _____

    _____

    _____

Day and Night and
How They Came To Be

Directions: Read the following poem. Be prepared to discuss how the Eskimo explains the natural environment.

Day and Night and How They Came To Be

In those times
when just saying a word
could make something happen,
there was no light on Earth yet.
Everything was in darkness all the time;
people lived in darkness.

A fox and a hare had an argument,
each saying his magic word:
"Darkness," said the fox,
for he wanted it to be dark so he could go hunting.

"Day," said the hare
for he wanted daylight
so he could find good grass to eat.

The hare won: His word was the more powerful
and he got his wish:
Day came, replacing night.
But the word of the fox was powerful too
and when day was over, night came,
and from then on they took turns with each other,
the nighttime of the fox
following the daytime of the hare.

Other Resources for Teaching with
Julie of the Wolves

Books

Butzow, Carol M. and John W. *Intermediate Science Through Children's Literature: Over Land and Sea.* Teacher Ideas Press, Englewood, CO, 1994. ISBN 0-8728-7946-1. Contains science lessons based upon *Julie of the Wolves, Sarah, Plain and Tall,* and *The Cay,* as well as other well-known books.

Cary, Alice. *Jean Craighead George: Meet the Author Series.* The Learning Works, 1996. ISBN 0-8816-0283-3.

Julie of the Wolves—Island of the Blue Dolphin Curriculum. Center for Learning, 1996. ISBN 1-5607-7282-4. Contains curriculum ideas and activities for both of these books.

Julie y Los Lobos/Julie of the Wolves. Demo Media, 1995. ISBN 0-6061-0431-3. The book in Spanish can be special-ordered at Amazon on-line bookstore: http://www.Amazon.com

Latitudes—Julie of the Wolves. Perfection Learning Company, PFF469-98, available from Social Studies School Service. Reproducible resource book that integrates social studies with literature and language arts. Contains activities based on *Julie of the Wolves.*

Web Sites

http://montana.avicom.net/ceri/jcg

Jean Craighead George's Home Page. This site contains a map pinpointing where the books take place, information on writing your own stories, and links to *Julie of the Wolves* and *Julie's Wolfpack.*

http://www.bev.net/education/schools/ces/frmocean.html

Contains a fifth-grade science curriculum based on literature including *Julie of the Wolves.* The lessons deal with the effect of temperature on states of matter and is based upon the State of Virginia Standards of Learning.

http://www.indiana.edu/~eric_rec/ieo/bibs/george.html

From the ERIC Clearinghouse, lists of bibliographies about author Jean Craighead George as well as links to other Web sites about the author.

http://sunrise.byu.edu/~browna/montessori/calder.html

Cathe Calder of the Meadow Montessori School in Monroe, Michigan, has put together an integrated curriculum for grades 1–8 using literature to teach themes in history, geography, and science. *Julie of the Wolves* is included.

http://www.innu.ca/

The Innuit Home Page contains information about Innuit history and culture. In both French and English.

TEACHER'S GUIDE

UNIT 4: *Maroo of the Winter Caves*
by Ann Turnbull

Turnbull, Ann. *Maroo of the Winter Caves.* New York: Clarion Books, 1984.

Description

Set during the Ice Age, this story relates how a young girl assumes adult responsibilities after the death of her father. The family belongs to a nomadic group of people who are journeying to their winter camp. Maroo's duty is to see her family to winter camp. She has responsibility for her grandmother, younger brother, mother, and her mother's baby.

Classroom Applications

The book is an "easy read" in that the language used is very appropriate for middle level learners. The story itself is engaging and spawns multiple methods for implementation. Of those mentioned in previous units, whole class reading and direct instruction seem to fit quite well. In this case, however, the students should take turns reading aloud. Be sure to have them read selections at night for homework. It is always good practice to have students read selections aloud only after they have had a chance to practice. This may eliminate any embarrassing situations.

To assist students through the book, they should complete a flow chart for each chapter they read. This will help them to organize their thinking and keep track of the story's progress. The reproducible flowchart on the following page can be photocopied for all of the students in your class for this purpose.

Maroo of the Winter Caves Flowchart

Directions: Complete this flowchart for each chapter of *Maroo of the Winter Caves* as you read the book.

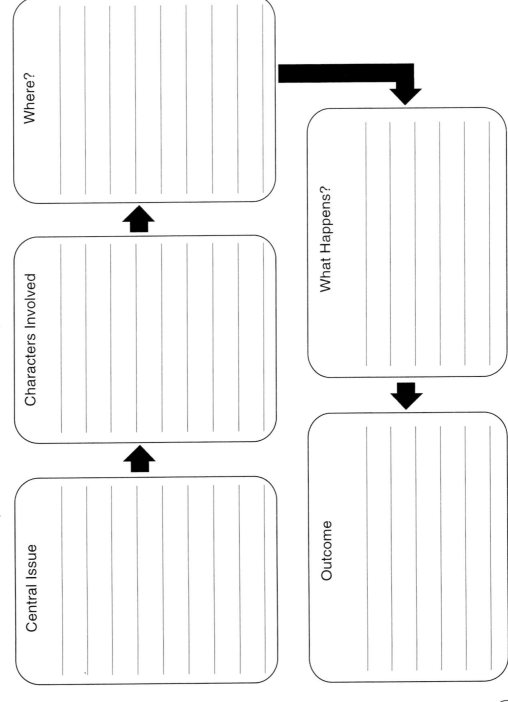

Where?

Characters Involved

Central Issue

What Happens?

Outcome

Lesson 1: Rise and Fall of the Great Lakes

Teacher's Lesson Plan

I. Time: one class period (45 minutes)

II. Frameworks/Standard Connection

Standard 4: the physical and human characteristics of places

Standard 7: the physical processes that shape the patterns of Earth's surface

III. Materials

- copy of the film/video *Rise and Fall of the Great Lakes* available from the Canadian National Film Board

- class sets of the Great Lakes Pretest and Human and Natural Changes in the Environment reproducible student worksheets 1A and 1B

IV. Objectives—Students will be able to:

- gather information from illustrative material

- identify, describe, and distinguish between natural and human changes to the environment

V. Procedures

1. Prepare students for the video by administering the Great Lakes Pretest student worksheet. Most of the answers to the pretest are common sense. The five Great Lakes (Huron, Ontario, Michigan, Erie, and Superior) spell the acronym HOMES. The lakes were created by the glacial action of the last Ice Age in North America 10,000 years ago. Evidence of the last Ice Age can be found in rock formations and "grooves" in the land. Cape Cod was deposited from Canada by the last glaciers.

2. Tell the students they will be watching a movie about how nature creates changes in the environment—in this case, in the formation of the Great Lakes. They will also see how humans have affected the environment—in the fall of the Great Lakes. The film is in two parts, the rise and the fall. In the first part, the camper in his canoe travels back in time to the last Ice Age. He bounces between past and present, pre- and post-Ice Age, throughout the first half of the film. In the second part, he is witness to changes made by humans in the building of the St. Lawrence Seaway.

3. Show the film to the students and ask them to record their observations on their Human and Natural Changes in the Environment worksheets. After viewing the film, have students volunteer their observations. A good conclusion to this activity is to have each student write a comparative essay describing the different changes wrought by nature and humans. Let them transfer their cryptic observations into an articulate essay.

Extension Activity The Ice Ages were not confined to the North American continent. Students can research the Ice Ages in Europe and Asia and compare them with the one depicted in the film.

Great Lakes Pretest

Directions: Prior to viewing the video *The Rise and Fall of the Great Lakes,* take the following pretest.

1. Define the term *environment.*

   _____

2. Name the five Great Lakes.

   _____

3. How do you think the Great Lakes were created?

   _____

   _____

4. When was the last Ice Age in North America?

   _____

5. What effects do you think the Ice Ages had on the environment? Did they have an effect on human habitation?

   _____

   _____

6. What evidence do you think there is of the last Ice Age? Are there any local examples?

   _____

   _____

Name _____ Date _____

Human and Natural Changes
in the Environment

Directions: As you view the video *The Rise and Fall of the Great Lakes*, complete this chart.

Changes Made by Nature	Changes Made by Humans

63   *Teaching Geography Through Literature*

Lesson 2: Maroo's Place

Teacher's Lesson Plan

I. **Time:** two to three class periods (45 minutes each)

II. **Frameworks/Standard Connection**

Standard 1: how to use maps and other geographic representations, tools, and technologies to acquire, process, and report information from a spatial perspective

Standard 3: how to analyze the spatial organization of people, places, and environments on Earth's surface

III. **Materials**

* the map on page *vi* of *Maroo of the Winter Caves*

* chart paper for each group of students

* class sets of Comparing Maps, Critical Sites, and The Environment reproducible student worksheets 2A, 2B, and 2C

* a map of contemporary France

* atlases

IV. **Objectives—Students will be able to:**

* create and interpret map symbols

* recognize climate patterns and characteristics

* make comparisons and draw conclusions from maps

V. **Procedures**

1. Remind the students about the content of the Author's Note on page *vii* of the book. Have them identify and locate the Massif Central, Maritime Alps, and Mediterranean Sea on their classroom maps of Europe.

2. Distribute the Comparing Maps student worksheet. Have students, together or in groups, complete the handout. Provide each group with chart paper and atlases.

3. After groups have completed the second activity, have them share observations in a whole class setting.

4. The third activity, identifying climatic characteristics, should be saved for an activity in an upcoming lesson (Cultural Considerations, in Lesson 3).

5. As students read through the book, they should identify the importance of the items on the Critical Sites student worksheet.

6. In order to establish a greater understanding of the differences between Ice Age and modern France, students should complete The Environment student worksheet. This may take some time as students read through the book as well as conduct research on their own.

Extension Activity In order to better visualize the differences in environment between modern France and Maroo's France, students can construct papier-maché physical maps of both.

Comparing Maps

Directions: As you work on your mapping assignment in class, complete the following activities.

1. The map on page *vi* of *Maroo of the Winter Caves* does not have a key. Create one in the space below. Be sure to use symbols for mountains, rivers, and place locations.

2. Turn to a map of Europe in your atlas. If possible, turn to a larger map of Western Europe and focus on France. What differences do you notice between the *Maroo* book's map and that of contemporary Europe? Your responses should focus on landforms, vegetation, and river systems. Remember, the location you are viewing is along the Mediterranean coast and near the Massif Central. Record your observations on the chart paper.

    _____

    _____

    _____

3. Locate a climate map of Europe. Concentrate on the climate of Central and Mediterranean France, the same area as the setting for the book. Identify the climatic characteristics of contemporary France. Record this information for future use.

Critical Sites

Directions: As you read through *Maroo of the Winter Caves*, identify the significance of the following:

Crossing Place of the Deer on the Great River _____

_____

White Mountain Trail _____

_____

Great Plain _____

_____

Summer Mountains _____

_____

Sea Camp _____

_____

The Snow House _____

_____

Pass of the Spirits _____

_____

Irimgadu _____

_____

Mountain Spirits _____

_____

Name _____ Date _____

The Environment

Directions: Maroo's environment is markedly different from today's environment in modern France. From your reading, list the different animals and resources available to Maroo. Next, use a series of maps of France from an atlas to discover the animal life and resources of modern France. Once you have done your research, answer the following questions.

1. Describe how people might live and work in Mediterranean France. How does this compare with Maroo's life and work?

   _____

   _____

   _____

   _____

   _____

2. Examine the map on page *vi* of the *Maroo* book. Using all the information you have gathered in all prior activities, suggest two reasons why the people of Ice Age times were nomadic and needed multiple camp sites depending on the time of year. Be sure to explain your reasons thoroughly.

   _____

   _____

   _____

   _____

   _____

Lesson 3: Your Thoughts

I.   **Time:** one to three class periods (45 minutes each)

II. **Frameworks/Standard Connection**

Standard 6—how culture and experience influence people's perceptions of places and regions

Standard 9—the characteristics, distribution, and migration of human populations on Earth's surface

Standard 10—the characteristics, distribution, and complexity of Earth's cultural mosaics

III. **Materials**

- class sets of Quotation Analysis and Cultural Considerations reproducible student worksheets 3A and 3B

IV. **Objectives—Students will be able to:**

- derive meaning about culture from printed text

- analyze elements of society relative to their significance

- articulate critically the importance of family structure and collaboration

V.   **Procedures**

1. Once the students have finished reading *Maroo*, distribute a copy of each activity sheet to them. You may choose to have the class work on the sheets in groups or individually, as homework or classwork. The questions are designed to address aspects of culture that can be generalized to other cultural explorations.

Extension Activity Students can prepare a collage representing the culture of Maroo's people. Many magazines have photographs and illustrations that are descriptive of the climate of Maroo's time.

Quotation Analysis

Directions: Please respond to these quotations from *Maroo of the Winter Caves*. Your opinions and responses must be supported by details. Draw upon all that you have researched during this unit as well as class discussions you may have had while reading the book.

1. "Areg began to sing. It was a short song about summer and the animals that could be hunted. The children stopped playing and gathered around. Everyone joined in the choruses and clapped the rhythm." *(page 31)* Given this passage, what part does song play in this culture? What about other cultures you may have studied?

   _____

   _____

   _____

   _____

2. "Then Maroo found the new drum, and the tears rushed to her eyes as she remembered the day they had celebrated its making. She offered it to Vorka, but he pushed it away. 'It will not speak to me,' he said. Reluctantly, Maroo laid the drum, too, into the grave." *(page 64)* Burial rights are an expression of a society's set of beliefs. How is this selection reflective of the religious beliefs of Maroo's people?

   _____

   _____

   _____

   _____

                       Teaching Geography Through Literature

Quotation Analysis *(continued)*

3. " 'The mountain hates us,' he said. 'It won't let me catch food.' " *(page 114)*
   Why does Otak ascribe his inability to catch game to the mountain?

   _____

   _____

   _____

   _____

   _____

4. "She remembered Old Mother's warning: there must be no risks taken; if one of them was lost or injured, the other must go on. One must survive." *(page 123)*
   The reasons for Old Mother's warning are pretty clear. But, is it right to give up searching for someone who is lost? We know what Maroo did. What would you do in this situation?

   _____

   _____

   _____

   _____

   _____

71   *Teaching Geography Through Literature*

Name _____   Date _____

UNIT 4, WORKSHEET 3B

Cultural Considerations

 Directions: After reading the book, consider the questions below. Each question will help you determine more about the culture of Maroo's people.

1. "Old Mother" is one of the prominent characters in the book. No decision is made without her advice and guidance. Using examples from your reading, illustrate her importance to the family group. What does Old Mother's role tell you about the structure of this society?

_____

_____

_____

_____

_____

_____

_____

2. There are many references in the book to "spirits." Citing three examples from your reading, explain the importance of these spirits. Describe the part they play in Maroo's culture.

_____

_____

_____

_____

_____

_____

_____

© 1999 J. Weston Walch, Publisher   72   *Teaching Geography Through Literature*

Cultural Considerations *(continued)*

3. Explain the relationship between Maroo's people and the environment. Support your reasoning with concrete examples from the book.

_____

_____

_____

_____

_____

_____

_____

4. Compare the feast described in Chapter 2 with modern-day feasts or festivals. What is the message communicated by the feast? What does it explain about the group's culture? Is this similar to anything you do?

_____

_____

_____

_____

_____

_____

_____

Cultural Considerations *(continued)*

5. The tools used by nomadic peoples needed to be portable but efficient. Identify some of the tools Maroo's people used. Compare them with their counterparts in today's modern era, including the materials used to create them and how the tools are employed.

_____

_____

_____

_____

_____

_____

6. Retrieve your climatic information from the Comparing Maps student worksheet. First, describe the climatic conditions of Maroo's time; then, compare the two sets of data. Put yourself in Maroo's place. What would you need to survive under such harsh conditions? Is there anywhere on Earth presently that experiences similar conditions to Maroo's?

_____

_____

_____

_____

_____

_____

Other Resources for Teaching with *Maroo of the Winter Caves*

Web Sites

http://www.sdcoe.k12.ca.us/score/maroo/marootg.htm

Teacher's guide to the teaching of *Maroo*—contains some great web links.

http://www.sdcoe.k12.ca.us/score/maroo/maroosg1.htm

A series of student activities based upon *Maroo of the Winter Caves* from the San Diego County Office of Education. Very inventive and well done. One activity takes the animals in the book and uses them ("Maroo's Zoo") to research prehistoric animals.

http://multimedia2.freac.fsu.edu/fga/academy/ascult.htm#activity2

A rich site containing activities on ancient peoples with an excellent bibliography. This site comes from the Geography Education and Technology Program at Florida State University. Check out their home page at http://multimedia2.freac.fsu.edu/ for geography lesson plans.

http://www.artsednet.getty.edu/ArtsEdNet/Resources/Erickson/Place/Supplements/Other/biblio.html

From the Getty Education Institute for the Arts, this site has a book list based upon an inquiry approach to art education called "Our Place in the World." It contains *Maroo*, other similar books, and some interesting approaches and lesson plans.

MacLachlan, Patricia. *Sarah, Plain and Tall*. New York: HarperCollins Children's Books, 1985. (ISBN 0-06-024101-2)

Description

Jacob Witting's wife died soon after giving birth to their son Caleb. This is the story of how Sarah Elisabeth Wheaton answered an advertisement and changed the lives of four people.

Classroom Applications

This is a very short book (58 pages), but it is full of history and geography. The details of prairie life contained within make excellent fodder for a comparative approach. For example, a standard lesson (see Lesson 2, Here, and Far Away) would be to compare the prairie (also known as "the breadbasket of the U.S.," "the Heartland," the "Upper Midwest," or the "North Central Region") with Maine or the New England states in terms of climate, resources, animal life, and vegetation.

Introduce the story as an example of historical reality, although this specific incident did not happen. Wives were often solicited by men via newspaper ads. The students should be informed that the book is as much a comparison between two ways of life (Midwestern and New England) as it is a geographic comparison.

To assist students through the book, they should complete a flowchart for each chapter they read. This will help them to organize their thinking and keep track of the story's progress. The reproducible flowchart on the following page can be photocopied for all of the students in your class for this purpose.

Name _____

Sarah, Plain and Tall Flowchart

Directions: Complete this flowchart for each chapter of *Sarah, Plain and Tall* as you read the book.

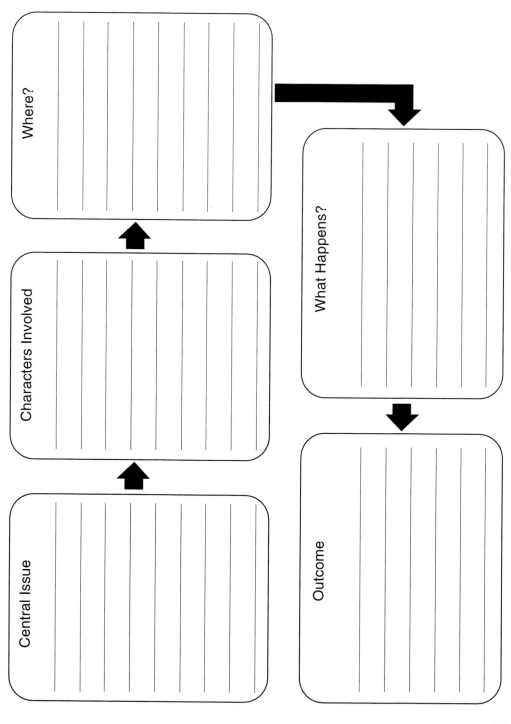

Central Issue

Characters Involved

Where?

What Happens?

Outcome

Lesson 1: States and Regions of the United States

I. **Time:** one class period (45 minutes) or homework

II. **Frameworks/Standard Connection**

Standard 1—how to use maps and other geographic representations, tools, and technologies to acquire, process, and report information from a spatial perspective

III. **Materials**

- class set of These Are the Places reproducible student worksheet 1A

- class set of atlases and outline map of the United States (p. 80)

IV. **Objectives—Students should be able to:**

- locate and identify states, regions, and physical features in the United States

V. **Procedures**

1. Prior to the students reading the book, this mapping exercise will help place the story in geographic context.

2. Distribute the United States political maps and the These Are the Places student worksheet. Have students complete the mapping exercise either as classwork or homework. Remind them to construct a key for their map, to include a compass rose, and to label neatly.

3. Collect the finished maps for review; return them to students for later use.

Name _____ Date _____

The Continental United States

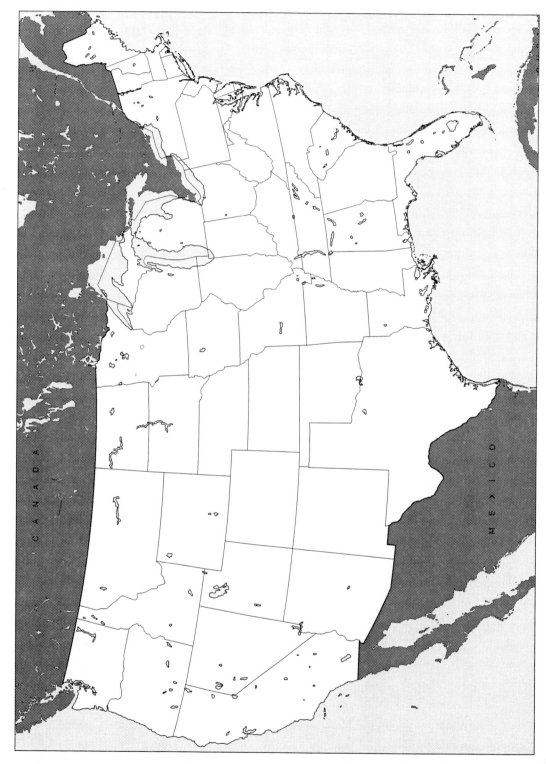

These Are the Places

Directions: Using your blank United States map and classroom atlases, locate, label, and color the following states. After locating each state, circle the New England and Prairie states.

North Dakota	Maine
South Dakota	New Hampshire
Minnesota	Vermont
Nebraska	Massachusetts
Kansas	Connecticut
Iowa	Rhode Island
Missouri	Tennessee

Next, label the following physical features. Color the mountains brown and the water bodies blue.

Atlantic Ocean	Pacific Ocean
Mississippi River	Missouri River
Appalachian Mountains	Ohio River
Rocky Mountains	Gulf of Mexico
Ozark Mountains	Arkansas River
Lake Michigan	Lake Erie
Lake Superior	Lake Ontario
Lake Huron	

Lesson 2: Here, and Far Away

Teacher's Lesson Plan

I. **Time:** one to four class periods (45 minutes each) depending on depth of research

II. **Frameworks/Standard Connection**

Standard 4—the physical and human characteristics of places

Standard 14—how human actions modify the physical environment

Standard 15—how physical systems affect human systems

Standard 16—the changes that occur in the meaning, use, distribution, and importance of resources

III. **Materials**

- class set of Comparing Regions reproducible student worksheet 2A

- class sets of population, land use, and agricultural products maps (pp. 83–85); an atlas or other resources containing transportation maps of the United States

IV. **Objectives—Students will be able to:**

- identify the economic activity of the prairie region, New England, and students' own locale

- draw conclusions about life in each of the regions

- interpret information from a variety of maps

V. **Procedures**

1. After the students have finished reading the book and reviewed the storyline, distribute the Comparing Regions student worksheet. The questions on this sheet are designed to enable students to draw comparisons and to distinguish among the regions. Some questions are historical in nature (#2); some are contemporary (#1, #3, #4, #5); and some apply to either historical or contemporary times (#2, #6). An interesting twist for question #5 would be to give students a historical map of the United States and ask them to draw conclusions based on history.

2. Once you have reviewed the assignment, you can have students complete it individually or collaboratively.

United States Population Density

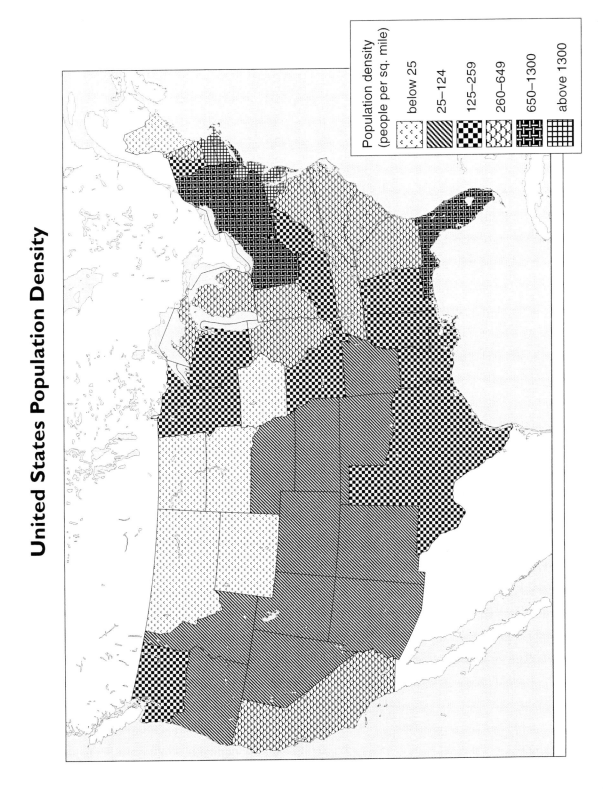

Population density
(people per sq. mile)

below 25

25–124

125–259

260–649

650–1300

above 1300

Teaching Geography Through Literature

Land Use in the Continental United States

Land Usage

cropland	
forest	
mountain region	
pasture	
wetland	
desert	

Teaching Geography Through Literature

Continental United States Agricultural Products

Legend:

tobacco		shellfish	maple syrup	cotton	sheep	cattle
vineyards		soybeans	peanuts	fishing	citrus fruits	pigs
wheat		timber	rice	fruit	corn	poultry

Name _____ Date _____

Comparing Regions

 Directions: Use your classroom atlases and your map handouts to answer the following questions about the United States. You may need to use additional resources to answer some of the questions.

1. What are the major crops grown in the following regions?

   The Prairie: _____

   New England: _____

   Your Locale: _____

2. What were the major transportation systems in place during the end of the nineteenth century in each region? How have these systems changed in the last hundred years?

   _____

   _____

   _____

   _____

3. Compare the population density of the three areas. What conclusions can you draw about settlement patterns?

   _____

   _____

   _____

   _____

(continued)

Comparing Regions *(continued)*

4. If you drove from Maine to South Dakota, what different kinds of agricultural products would you see?

_____

_____

_____

_____

5. Identify the largest cities in each of the states you located on your United States political map from the last lesson. Give reasons for the locations of these cities.

_____

_____

_____

_____

_____

_____

6. There are usually defining characteristics that unify places into a region. Using the maps and your reading of *Sarah, Plain and Tall*, identify the unifying features of:

The Prairie: _____

_____

New England: _____

_____

Lesson 3: Life on the Prairie; Life in New England

I. **Time:** one to two class periods (45 minutes each)

II. **Frameworks/Standard Connection**

   Standard 9—the characteristics, distribution, and migration of human populations on Earth's surface

III. **Materials**

   - class set of Looking at Differences and Similarities reproducible student worksheet 3A

IV. **Objectives—Students will be able to:**

   - make comparisons between New England and the Prairie

   - explain the conditions of life in each region

V. **Procedure**

   1. As a final exercise for this book, the Looking at Differences and Similarities worksheet provides a yardstick to measure student learning. A few questions are directly related to the book; others require some additional research.

Extension Activity Have students investigate the Native American cultures that first inhabited the regions currently under study. Through a bulletin board display, diorama, or collage, students can illustrate the similarities and differences among the cultures. A point of focus might be the environment and how each culture influenced and was influenced by it.

Looking at Differences and Similarities

 Directions: Answer the following questions using details from *Sarah, Plain and Tall* to support your conclusions. You may also need to consult other sources of information beyond the book. Use a separate sheet of paper for each question.

1. Investigate the homes of early settlers on the Prairie, such as sod houses, and compare them with the wood-frame homes of nineteenth-century New England. Include in your investigation the architecture, materials used, and carpentry methods.

2. Describe the life of the Witting family on the Prairie. Include in your observations the family's economic activity, use of available natural resources, entertainment, nearness of neighbors and the town, and food.

3. What was Sarah's life like in Maine? How did it change when she moved to the Witting's farm?

4. What do you think contributed to Sarah's decision to answer Jacob's advertisement? What considerations went into her decision to marry Jacob and remain on the farm?

Other Resources for Teaching with
Sarah, Plain and Tall

Books

McGowan, Tom and Meredith McGowan. *Telling America's Story: Teaching American History Through Children's Literature.* Milwaukee, WI, Jenson Publishers, 1989. Grades 4–8. Has lesson plans using fifteen works of literature including *Sarah, Plain and Tall.*

Miller, Wanda J. *U.S. History Through Children's Literature: From the Colonial Period to World War II.* Englewood, CO. Teacher Ideas Press, 1997. Grades 4–8. ISBN 1-5630-8440-6. Uses *Sarah* as one of the works of literature.

Web Sites

http://www.mcps.k12.md.us/curriculum/socialstd/grade5/Sarah_Plain.html

From the Montgomery County Schools in Rockville, Maryland, this site contains a synopsis of the book with economics and geography lessons.

Media Resources

"Sarah, Plain and Tall" Hallmark Hall of Fame, 1991, production starring Glenn Close as Sarah. 98 minutes. Available either in VHS videotape format or CLV Laserdisc. Available from Zenger Media, 10200 Jefferson Boulevard, Room 95, P.O. Box 802, Culver City, CA 90232-0802. 1-800-421-4246.

"Skylark" Hallmark Hall of Fame, 1992, sequel to "Sarah, Plain and Tall." 98 minutes. Available in VHS video format from Zenger Media.

Hansen, Joyce. *The Captive.* New York: Scholastic Press, 1994. (ISBN 0-5904-1625-1)

Description

Historical fiction based on the real-life story of Gustavus Vassa, an African. This is the story of an Ashanti family that is captured in West Africa and sold into slavery. Koffi, the young son, finds himself on a New England farm. In this saga, Koffi discovers an African-American shipbuilder whose goal is to help Africans return to their homeland. This book is a comprehensive account of eighteenth-century slave trade and the effect it had on captured Africans.

Classroom Applications

A perfect complement to any United States history or world geography course, *The Captive* is an ideal vehicle through which to teach African geography and the geography of the slave trade. While the majority of the following lessons are separate from the text of *The Captive,* connections can be made to the text. For example, the first lesson, "African Art on the World Wide Web," offers opportunities to explore a variety of African civilizations established prior to European slave trade. This exercise will provide insight into the existing cultures of Africa, including those of West Africa. The activities can be done either in tandem with reading the book or as preparatory lessons before reading.

Students should complete a flowchart for each chapter they read. This will help them organize their thinking and keep track of the story's progress. The reproducible flowchart on the following page can be photocopied for all of the students in your class for this purpose.

The Captive Flowchart

Directions: Complete this flowchart for each chapter of *The Captive* as you read the book.

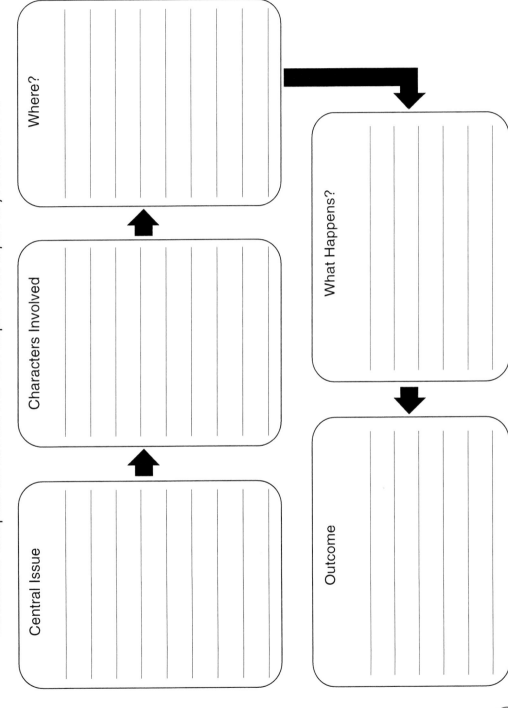

Central Issue

Characters Involved

Where?

What Happens?

Outcome

Lesson 1: African Art on the World Wide Web

I. **Time:** one class period (45 minutes)

II. **Frameworks/Standard Connection**

Standard 6—how culture and experience influence people's perceptions of places and regions

Standard 10—the characteristics, distribution, and complexity of Earth's cultural mosaics

III. **Materials**

- class set of African Art—What Does It Have to Tell You? reproducible student worksheet 1A

- computer stations (1 for every 2–3 students) connected to the Internet

IV. **Objectives—Students will be able to:**

- access information on the World Wide Web

- critically analyze art work

- draw conclusions from analysis of art work

- work in teams cooperatively

V. **Procedures**

1. Before the lesson, bookmark the Web sites listed on the worksheet on each computer station. As of summer 1999, these are all active sites. You can also add any appropriate Web sites you find through your own research.

2. Review with students your school's policies regarding the use of computers and Internet research.

3. Introduce the lesson by reviewing the worksheet with the class. Remind students to use only those sites that you have bookmarked on the computers. Then, create teams to conduct the investigation. While students are pursuing their research, circulate among the teams to monitor their progress.

4. When all groups have finished, provide time for each group to report its findings, particularly regarding questions 6 and 8.

African Art—
What Does It Have to Tell You?

Directions: Your task for this assignment is to locate an example of African art from one of the Web sites given below or given by your teacher. Examine the artwork, answer the questions below, and see what conclusions you can draw from your investigation.

Web Sites

African Art: Aesthetics and Meaning

http://www.lib.virginia.edu/dic/exhib/93.ray.aa/African.html

National Museum of African Art

http://www.si.edu/organiza/museums/africart/nmfa.htm

DIA Galleries—African Art

http://www.dia.org/galleries/aonwc/africanart/africanart.html

Hamill Gallery of African Art

http://www.tiac.net/users/thamill/

1. Name of the artwork: _____

2. Type (sculpture, mask, etc.): _____

3. Civilization it's from: _____

(continued)

African Art—
What Does It Have to Tell You? (continued)

4. Date that it was made: _____

5. Purpose it was made for: _____

    _____

6. After careful observation, write ten words or phrases to describe the artwork you have chosen.

    _____

    _____

    _____

    _____

7. Why did you choose this particular piece of artwork?

    _____

    _____

    _____

    _____

8. Pretend you are part of a team of archaeologists uncovering this art for the first time. What does this piece of art tell you about the civilization that made it?

    _____

    _____

    _____

    _____

Lesson 2: African Geography

I. **Time:** one or two class periods (45 minutes each)

II. **Frameworks/Standard Connection**

Standard 1—how to use maps and other geographic representations, tools, and technologies to acquire, process, and report information from a spatial perspective

Standard 2 —how to use mental maps to organize information about people, places, and environments in a spatial context

Standard 3—how to analyze the spatial organization of people, places, and environments on Earth's surface

III. **Materials**

- two class sets of physical maps of Africa; one class set of political map of Africa (pp. 99–100)

- classroom atlases

- colored pencils/crayons

- class sets of The Physical Landscape of Africa, African Climatic Patterns, The Political Landscape of Africa, and Using the Maps reproducible student worksheets 2A–2D

IV. **Objectives—Students will be able to:**

- read, analyze, and interpret information from a variety of maps (climatic, physical, political)

- identify the countries of West Africa, major rivers, physical features, and climatic patterns

- draw conclusions from graphic illustrations

V. **Procedures**

1. As an introduction to *The Captive,* have students complete the following activities as either homework, classwork, or a combination of both.

2. Distribute the maps and worksheets and review them with the students. Have students complete them as either classwork or homework.

Extension Activity Students should research the river systems of Africa. They will need a variety of Africa maps to address research questions. How and why do rivers begin in certain areas of Africa? What is unique about the physical landscape of Africa, and how do those factors influence its river systems?

Name _____ Date _____

Blank Physical Map of Africa

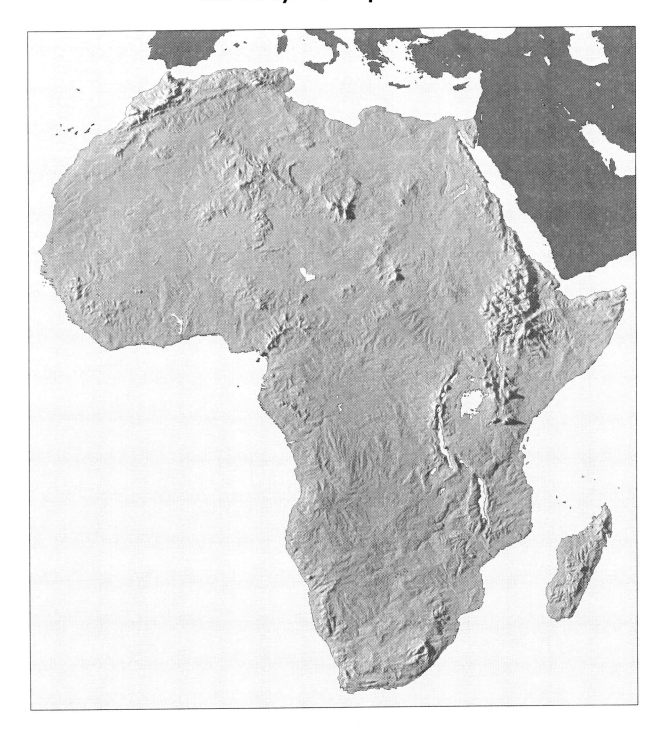

Name _____ Date _____

Blank Political Map of Africa

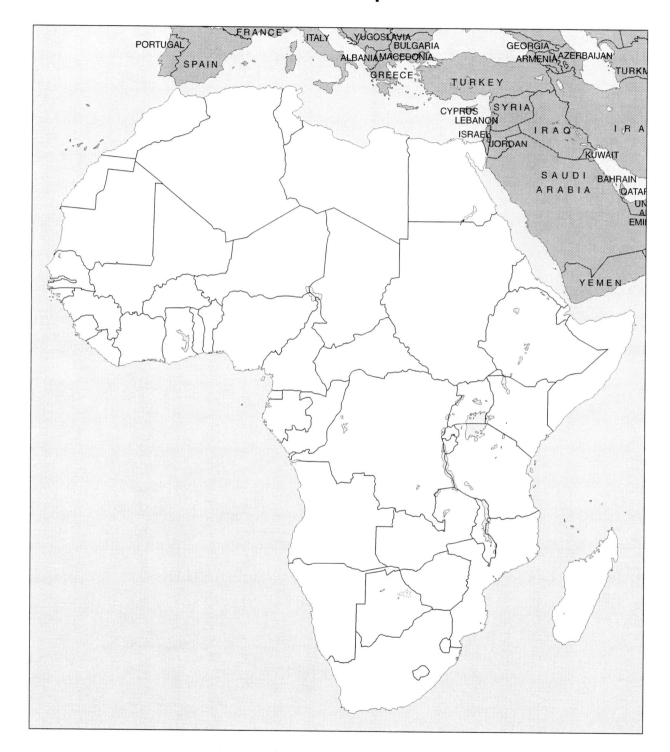

Teaching Geography Through Literature

The Physical Landscape of Africa

Directions: On your blank physical map of Africa, locate and label the following features.

Landforms	Bodies of Water
Atlas Mountains	Niger River
Namib Desert	Lake Victoria
Sahara Desert	Nile River
Mount Kilimanjaro	Atlantic Ocean
Libyan Desert	Indian Ocean
Cape of Good Hope	Lake Tanganyika
Cape Palmas	Lake Albert
Ahaggar Mountains	Lake Volta
The Horn	Senegal River
Ethiopian Highlands	Orange River
Cape Verde	Zambesi River
Grain Coast	Gambia River
Ivory Coast	Ubangi River
Gold Coast	Gulf of Guinea
Slave Coast	Mediterranean Sea

African Climatic Patterns

 Directions: On your second blank physical map of Africa, locate, label, and color the climatic regions of Africa listed below.

Desert	Mediterranean
Savanna	Steppe
Tropical Rain Forest	Marine West Coast

Research average monthly temperatures and precipitation during a calendar year for any of the cities listed on Worksheet 2C. In the space below or on graph paper, create a climograph using this information. Identify the specific climate of the city selected.

         Teaching Geography Through Literature

The Political Landscape of Africa

 Directions: Identify and locate the following West African countries and cities. Add them to your blank political map of Africa.

Countries	Cities
Senegal	Dakar
Gabon	Libreville
Guinea	Conarky
Sierra Leone	Freetown
Nigeria	Abuja
Benin	Porto Novo
Togo	Cote D'Ivoire
Liberia	Monrovia
Gambia	Banjul
Equatorial Guinea	Malabo
Guinea-Bissau	Bissau
Cameroon	Yaounde
Burkina Faso	Ouagadougou
Sao Tome and Principe	Sao Tome

Using the Maps

 Directions: Using the maps you have prepared as well as precipitation and population maps of Africa, answer the following questions.

1. What characteristics of the west coast of Africa encouraged slave traders to establish ports there?

   _____

   _____

   _____

2. Based upon the data from all the maps, what conclusions can you draw about the distribution of population in Africa?

   _____

   _____

   _____

3. Using climatic and precipitation data, describe the differences in living conditions between Senegal and Gabon.

   _____

   _____

   _____

   _____

Teaching Geography Through Literature

Lesson 3: Before European Slave Trade

Teacher's Lesson Plan

I. **Time:** one to four class periods (45 minutes each)

II. **Frameworks/Standard Connection**

Standard 4—the physical and human characteristics of places

Standard 5—that people create regions to interpret Earth's complexity

Standard 6—how culture and experience influence people's perceptions of places and regions

III. **Materials**

- library and historical reference materials for Africa prior to European slave trade

- class set of Investigating Fifteenth-Century Africa reproducible student worksheet 3A

- chart paper for recording student research

IV. **Objectives—Students will be able to:**

- identify various aspects of African civilizations

- describe life in West Africa during the fifteenth century

- conduct research, organize material, and communicate information

- work collaboratively in groups

V. **Procedures**

1. Advise students that this exercise will focus on fifteenth-century Africa. Point out that the political geography of Africa then was very different from that of Africa today.

2. Divide the class into six research groups:

   Group 1—Family and Social Life

   Group 2—Economic Activities

   Group 3—Kingdom of Ghana

   Group 4—Kingdom of Mali

   Group 5—Kingdom of Songhay

   Group 6—The Ashanti

3. Assign each group a particular area in the room in which to conduct research. Distribute materials and supplies. Students should complete the research within two class periods and spend one class period creating the poster.

4. Have each group orally present its findings.

Investigating Fifteenth-Century Africa

Directions: Your group's assignment is to use the available materials to research a specific aspect of West African society in the fifteenth century. As you conduct your research, focus on the questions outlined below.

1. **Family and Social Life**

   • What role did the extended family play in West African society?

   • How did religion act as a controlling force?

   • In what ways was African slavery different from European slavery?

2. **Economic Activities**

   • What forms of agriculture were practiced?

   • How did West Africans exchange goods and services?

   • What was the African concept of property ownership?

3. **The Three Great Kingdoms (Ghana, Mali, and Songhay) and the Ashanti**

   • When was each empire at its zenith?

   • What were the major contributions of each?

   • How was each organized politically?

   • What factors led to the decline of each?

After completing your research, create a poster using chart paper to visually communicate your findings. You may use pictures from magazines or drawings to enhance your poster.

Lesson 4: The Geography of African Slavery

I. **Time:** one to three class periods (45 minutes each)

II. **Frameworks/Standard Connection**

Standard 1—how to use maps and other geographic representations, tools, and technologies to acquire, process, and report information from a spatial perspective

Standard 3—how to analyze the spatial organization of people, places, and environments on Earth's surface

Standard 9—the characteristics, distribution, and migration of human populations on Earth's surface

Standard 11— the patterns and networks of economic interdependence on Earth's surface

III. **Materials**

- two class sets of outline maps of the Atlantic Basin (p. 110)

- rulers, pencils, colored pencils

- classroom atlases

- class sets of Slave Trade and Perspectives reproducible student worksheets 4A and 4B

IV. **Objectives—Students will be able to:**

- identify the routes of the slave trade from Africa

- derive information from maps and draw conclusions from the information

- use maps to communicate information

V. **Procedures**

1. Announce to students that they will be exploring the geography of the African slave trade by using maps and deriving information from them.

2. Explain to the class that the European trading in African slaves lasted for more than 300 years. Africans were bought and sold into slavery throughout the Americas. They were traded for guns, textiles, and alcohol in Africa. In the Americas, they were traded for gold, silver, tobacco, and sugar.

3. Distribute the outline maps of the Atlantic Basin and the Slave Trade worksheets. Tell students to follow the directions while completing the map work. Collect the completed maps and use them as displays around the room.

4. Distribute the Perspectives student worksheet. Explain the purpose of the exercise—students are to view the issue of slavery from different perspectives. Divide the class into five groups.

5. When students have completed the exercise, have them share responses.

The Atlantic Basin

Slave Trade

Directions: Use both of your maps of the Atlantic Basin and classroom atlases to complete this exercise.

1. On one of the maps, locate and label the following present-day African countries:

Senegal	Gambia
Guinea	Sierra Leone
Liberia	Ghana
Togo	Benin
Nigeria	Cameroon
Equatorial Guinea	Gabon
Angola	Namibia

2. Locate and label the following places in North and South America:

Brazil	Nicaragua
Colombia	French Guiana
Greater Antilles	Virginia, U.S.

3. Draw the following slave trade routes:

• from Namibia/Angola to Brazil (route 1 in red)

• from the rest of the listed countries in #1 to Virginia (route 2 in green); to French Guiana (route 3 in orange); to Colombia and Nicaragua (route 4 in yellow)

(continued)

Slave Trade *(continued)*

4. For each of the routes, determine the distance in miles or kilometers.

   Route 1 _____   Route 2 _____

   Route 3 _____   Route 4 _____

5. On your second map of the Atlantic Basin, locate and label New England, the Gold and Slave Coasts, and the Antilles. Draw a line in black linking New England with the Slave and Gold Coasts. Then, connect the Gold and Slave Coasts with the Antilles. Finally, connect the Antilles to New England. You have just drawn the route of the New England Triangular Trade. Take time to research this trading route, focusing on what was traded on each leg of the triangle.

   New England to Africa _____

   _____

   _____

   _____

   Africa to the Antilles _____

   _____

   _____

   _____

   The Antilles to New England _____

   _____

   _____

   _____

     Teaching Geography Through Literature

Perspectives

Directions: Your class has been divided into five groups. Each group will assume your assigned role. Base your responses to the following numbered statements from your character's perspective. Be sure to consider whether there are benefits or not for the group that you represent. Use your reading of *The Captive*, knowledge of U.S. history, and information gathered during the previous activities.

Group 1—Africans	Group 4—American Citizens
Group 2—African Slaves	Group 5—Plantation Owners
Group 3—Slave Traders	

1. Slavery is profitable for me.

   _____

   _____

2. I can accept slavery under certain conditions.

   _____

   _____

3. Slavery should be abolished.

   _____

   _____

Lesson 5: *The Captive*

I. **Time:** two to four class periods (45 minutes each)

II. **Frameworks/Standard Connection**

Standard 6—how culture and experience influence people's perceptions of places and regions

Standard 9—the characteristics, distribution, and migration of human populations on Earth's surface

Standard 10—the characteristics, distribution, and complexity of Earth's cultural mosaics

Standard 11—the patterns and networks of economic interdependence on Earth's surface

Standard 13—how the forces of cooperation and conflict among people influence the division and control of Earth's surface

Standard 17—how to apply geography to interpret the past

III. **Materials**

- copy of *The Captive* for each student

- class sets of Considering the Flowcharts and Alternative Presentations reproducible student worksheets 5A and 5B

- 21 copies of Group Work—*The Captive* Flowchart for each group

IV. **Objectives—Students will be able to:**

- work collaboratively to share knowledge, make decisions, and communicate ideas

- make inferences and draw conclusions from textual material

- analyze and articulate the major themes of the book

V. Procedures

1. This activity is to be implemented after the students have completed reading *The Captive*. As students complete the flowcharts for each chapter, you should collect, review, and return them. The students will need corrected flowcharts for this exercise.

2. Divide the class into groups of four or five students each.

3. Distribute the Considering the Flowcharts and Group Work—*The Captive* Flowchart student worksheets.

4. Student groups should complete one flowchart for each chapter, then address the questions and statements found on the Considering the Flowcharts student worksheet.

5. As a culminating activity, the groups are to retell the story using the options found on the Alternative Presentations worksheet.

Considering the Flowcharts

Directions: By this time, you should have a collection of 21 flowcharts. Working together as a group, complete one collective flowchart for each of the chapters. Then, consider the questions listed below on a separate sheet of paper.

1. Who are the main characters of the book?

2. Describe the setting (location, time, geography) of Kofi's location in Africa.

3. Describe the characteristics of Ashanti culture as revealed in the book.

4. Explain the major episodes in Kofi's life. What happened to him during his journey to America? What was America like when he arrived?

5. How did Kofi cope with American culture?

6. What, in your opinion, are the primary themes of this book?

7. What thoughts and emotions do you think Kofi is experiencing?

Group Work—The Captive Flowchart

Directions: As a group, complete this flowchart for each chapter of *The Captive*.

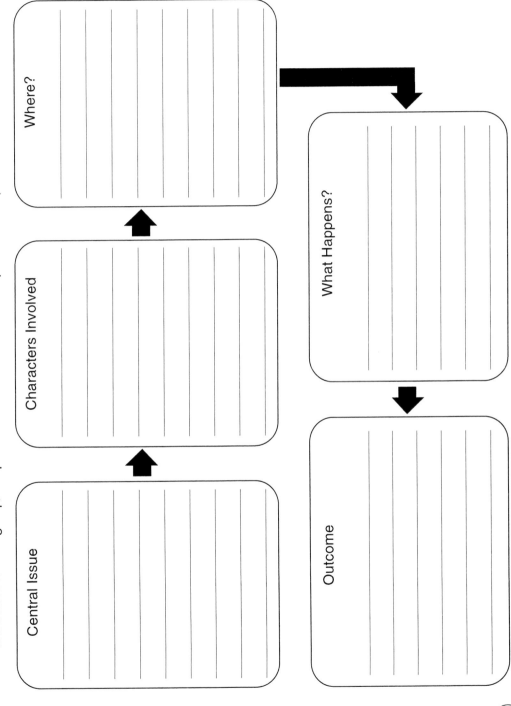

Where?

Characters Involved

Central Issue

What Happens?

Outcome

Alternative Presentations

 Directions: Choose one of the presentation formats listed below. Then, as a group, present to the class your responses to the book and to the previous questions on worksheet 5A.

- Conduct a panel discussion whose participants include a slave trader, an African slave, a Southern plantation owner, and a moderator.

- Choose an episode from the book and reenact it for the class.

- Debate the following resolution:
  "Slavery was necessary for the economic development of the Southern colonies."

- Portray a slave ship crew. Recount the conditions on board ship and the treatment of the "cargo."

- Assume the role of one of the characters (other than Kofi) in the book. Explain your actions to the "audience."

- You are members of the Ashanti society, and you have just met the first European slave trader. Communicate your society's feelings about slavery.

Other Resources for Teaching with
The Captive

Since the publication date of *The Captive* is so recent, there are not many sites that reference this work directly. Teachers are encouraged to search on their own as this book gains more frequent use in classrooms.

Books

Day, Frances Ann. *Multicultural Voices in Contemporary Literature: A Resource for Teachers.* Heineman Press, Portsmouth, 1994. ISBN 0-4350-8826-2. This book has other titles by Joyce Hansen, as well as additional sources for multicultural literature.

Linquist, Tarry. "Why and How I Teach With Historical Fiction," *Instructor,* August 14, 1997. An article on teaching strategies with *The Captive* as well as fourteen other books.

Resources for Teachers

The list of books and Web sites on young adult literature and geography literally changes daily. The sources listed below will be jumping-off points for your own personal research and should provide some guidance and ideas about using literature to teach Geography and other Social Studies material.

> Two recommended search engines on the World Wide Web that seem to yield the best results for teachers are AltaVista (http://altavista.digital.com/) and Northern Light (http://www.nlsearch.com).

Books

Altmann, Patricia and Lisa Luciano. *Ready-To-Use Literature Activities for Grades 7–12.* Prentice Hall Trade Books, New York, 1988. ISBN 0-8762-8778-8.

Bannister, Sharon and Twyla R. Wells. *Teaching American History Through the Novel.* J. Weston Walch, Portland, ME, 1995. ISBN 0-8251-2746-7. This reproducible teacher book for grades 6–12 outlines more than 300 novels and contains 51 activities for using literature to teach U.S. History.

Bednarz, Sarah Witham, et al. *Geography for Life.* National Geographic Research and Exploration, Washington, DC, 1994. ISBN 0-7922-2775-1

Bishop, Rudine Sims, ed. *Kaleidoscope: A Multicultural Booklist for Grades K–8.* National Council of Teachers of English, Urbana, 1994. ISBN 0-8141-2543-3.

Helms, Bonnie. *150 Great Books: Synopses, Quizzes, and Tests for Independent Reading.* J. Weston Walch, Portland, ME, 1986. ISBN 0-8251-0117-4. Classic works of literature arranged by theme and degree of difficulty for students in grades 7–12. This is designed to help teachers prepare and evaluate independent reading assignments. There is also a sequel to this titled *100 More Great Books,* which contains additional titles and is available from the same publisher.

Irvin, Judith L., et al. *Enhancing Social Studies Through Literacy Strategies.* Bulletin No. 91. National Council for the Social Studies, Washington, DC, 1995. ISBN 0-8978-6067-7.

McElmeel, Sharron L. *Adventures with Social Studies (Through Literature).* Libraries Unlimited, Englewood, CO, 1991. ISBN 0-8728-7828-7.

Kemball, Walter G., ed. *Spaces and Places: A Geography Manual for Teachers.* Rand McNally Educational Publishing Division, Skokie, IL, 1995. ISBN 0-5281-7899-9.

Natoli, Salvatore, ed. *Strengthening Geography in the Social Studies.* Bulletin No. 81. National Council for the Social Studies, Washington, DC, 1994. ISBN 0-87986-056-1.

Sawyer, Walter, Diana E. Comer, and Sally Newcomb. *Growing Up with Literature.* Delmar Publishers, Albany, NY, 1995. ISBN 0-8273-4340-0.

Selwyn, Douglas. *Arts and Humanities in the Social Studies.* Bulletin 90. National Council for the Social Studies, Washington, DC, 1995. ISBN 0-8798-6064-2.

Wood, Monica. *12 Multicultural Novels: Reading and Teaching Strategies.* J. Weston Walch, Portland, ME, 1997. Study units for books by authors from diverse cultures for grades 6–12. ISBN 0-8251-2901-X.

Web Sites

http://multimedia2.freac.fsu.edu/ncge/

The National Council for Geographic Education's home page with information about resources and conferences.

http://www.nationalgeographic.com/main.html

The National Geographic Society's home page is an excellent site with a link to a section on geography education.

http://atla.library.vanderbilt.edu/education/childlit.html

Site from Vanderbilt University that specializes in children's and young adult literature. It has links to a teacher resource center, which includes plans for teaching with literature.

http://ericir.sunsite.syr.edu/

ERIC is the Educational Resources Information Center, a federally funded national information system about education. There is an abundance of information from articles about education to sample lessons.